SHAKEN
FOUNDATIONS

SHAKEN FOUNDATI●NS

THEOLOGICAL FOUNDATIONS FOR MISSION

PETER BEYERHAUS

ZONDERVAN PUBLISHING HOUSE

A DIVISION OF THE ZONDERVAN CORPORATION

GRAND RAPIDS, MICHIGAN

45541

TO

DONALD McGAVRAN

THIS BOOK IS DEDICATED

WITH APPRECIATION AND RESPECT

Contents

foreword

These Church Growth Lectures, delivered in the Spring of 1972, clearly reflect their author's uncommon combination of interest and background. Peter Beyerhaus is missionary, scholar, churchman, and theologian. Each facet of his training and practice shines through these chapters.

As theologian, he has tackled the tensions in the field of biblical interpretation, tensions that seek to pull the Church away from the Reformation's commitment to the authority of Scripture alone. With keen insight he has noted the connection between the Church's view of biblical authority and its engagement in mission. Both the higher criticism of the late nineteenth century and its more recent offspring in the writings of Bultmann and his followers have had a decidedly negative impact on the Church's outreach to those who do not honor Christ's name. Though his illustrations are largely German, they are not wasted on us Americans. The same trends are present with us, if only because theology in America has been so dependent on Germany.

As churchman and theologian, he has sounded sharp warning about the course charted by the World Council of Churches. I sat through the long debates at Uppsala, when delegates and consultants tried to hammer out an acceptable and viable definition of mission. The frustrations he expresses, I felt. The reluctance to talk about man's lostness, the glib desire to apply the traits of the New Humanity for all men regardless of their faith in Jesus Christ, the tendency to highlight man's physical, social, economic and political needs, while leaving his need for reconciliation to God in dim shadow—all this conspired to make Uppsala an uncomfortable experience. And ecumenical pronouncements in the four years since Uppsala have done little to ease our frustrations.

It is against this backdrop that we must see the Frankfurt Declaration. At a time when ambivalence seemed the best we could expect from any conclave of European Christians, a clear note rang forth, a clear note calling with urgency in evangelism as well as constancy in social concerns. As a key participant in the Theological Convention held at Frankfurt in 1970, Professor Beyerhaus is in a unique position to sketch the background and assess the importance of the Declaration, to which too little attention has yet been paid in the United States.

Professor Beyerhaus' criticisms of the ecumenical movement may seem stern to some, but at the same time his judgments will seem balanced. He is not a militant separatist ready to drum out of the corps churchmen whose opinions clash with his. His is not a narrow view of mission, devoid of social responsibility. The chapter on Missions and Racism beats with the pulse of a man who deeply resents bigotry, prejudice, and racism. Firsthand he has seen all of these in his missionary service in South Africa. Politics, piety, and proclamation are means that he urges to deal with these affronts to the Christian gospel. Where the faith has had too little effect on social change, the fault lies not in the gospel but in our reluctance to believe whole-heartedly in its power and its demands.

Despite their stark analysis of the directions of much ecumenical thought about missions, these lectures give me hope. Not only do they call for a return to biblical authority and a dependence on the Holy Spirit, but they demonstrate what they call for. What helps me to hope is the thought that Professor Beyerhaus and his colleagues will have an impact on evangelism and missions in the German Lutheran Church akin to that of Inter Varsity Christian Fellowship and men like John Stott, Marcus Loane, and Leon Morris in the Anglican communion of England and Australia. It is with that hope that I commend these lectures on mission to a believing Church in America and beyond.

David Allan Hubbard
President, Fuller
Theological Seminary

August, 1972.

Preface

The occasion for Peter Beyerhaus' first visit to the United States was an invitation from Dean Emeritus Donald McGavran of the Fuller Theological Seminary School of Missions to deliver the annual Church Growth Lectures there. Beyerhaus' name had become well-known and highly respected among evangelicals in this country in 1970 as a result of the publication in *Church Growth Bulletin* and *Christianity Today* of the Courageous "Frankfurt Declaration on the Fundamental Crisis in Christian Mission." The story behind this key document is given in all its detail for the first time in Chapter 5. When Beyerhaus' book, *Missions, Which Way?* began to circulate last year, his status as one of today's outstanding evangelical missiologists was confirmed.

The 1972 Church Growth Lectures, published under the title, *Shaken Foundations, Theological Foundations for Mission,* comprise one of the clearest cases for biblical theology of mission available in print. When Beyerhaus concluded his lectures in Pasadena, McGavran commented as follows:

> Throughout his lectures he was exposing to public view the tremendous shift from great commission missions to social action missions, from missions working for vertical reconciliation with God to those working for horizontal reconciliation of men with men. He set forth the depth and seriousness of the changes advocated in some quarters and exposed their theological roots.

From Fuller Seminary, Beyerhaus moved on to speak at Trinity Evangelical Divinity School, Wheaton College, Concordia Seminary in St. Louis, Lincoln Christian College, Luther Seminary, Gordon-Conwell Seminary, and the Protestant Episcopal Seminary in Virginia. His address to the Evangelical Foreign Missions Association annual meetings in St. Louis was acclaimed by mission executives as one of the clearest and most encouraging theological lectures they had heard in many a year. All in all, Beyerhaus returned to his Chair of Missions at the University of Tübingen with a well-deserved feeling of satisfaction that God had used him to make a substantial contribution to the expansion of the cause of evangelical missions in the United States.

I personally felt highly honored when Peter Beyerhaus asked me to edit his lectures and see to their publication. Being close to him and to his thinking has been a rewarding experience. I am confident it will be equally rewarding to the readers of this book.

Two of the chapters have been previously published in unrevised form, and acknowledgment is in order. When Chapter 2 appeared under the title "Confessing Protestantism in West Germany," in the July 7, 1972, issue of *Christianity Today,* Editor Harold Lindsell commented, "We regard this as one of the most significant and provocative essays we have published this year." Chapter 4 was originally published as "Mission and Humanization" in the January, 1971, issue of *International Review of Mission* and is included with permission.

— C. PETER WAGNER

Pasadena, California
July, 1972

SHAKEN
FOUNDATIONS

1

Biblical Hermeneutics
The Starting Point

A few years ago Christians in Germany were stirred up by the appearance of a book with the provocative title, *Alarm About the Bible.* The reason for publishing this bestseller was not so much that academic theologians had begun to question the authenticity of many biblical texts. What worried the author was rather that higher critics had started to propogate the results of their research among ordinary Christians. This they did through popular literature, radio and television. In view of these determined efforts of modernist theology to intrude deeply into the Christian community, Dr. Bergmann wrote, "The Alarm must be sounded to the followers of Jesus."

The adherents of modernist theology, however, continued their campaign enthusiastically. They regarded it almost as a missionary endeavor. They pressed forward rapidly and thoroughly with a barrage of information launched on the broadest possible scale. They maintained that the Church during past decades had heaped upon itself a great burden of guilt by neglecting to inform its members of the important results of literary, historic and textual criticism of the Bible. Thus, they insisted, Christians were kept in a stage of immaturity and even childish belief. The modernists held that the Church had closed off the Gospel to people who are unable to combine their childish belief with sound reason.

Thus in the same Church two groups confronted each other in regard to biblical criticism. One group regarded the process as detrimental to the congregation; the other regarded it as educative and evangelistic.

In this chapter I do not hide behind the bush or retreat to the golden middle way. Rather, from the outset I confess that I share the deep concern of Dr. Bergmann. But I do not want to limit myself to sounding an alarm. I want to attempt to go further down and expose some other basic issues.

THE BIBLE AT THE CENTER

The *Sola Scriptura* Principle of the Reformation.

The battle about the Bible which rages at present in several Western countries is not simply a case of scholastic hair-splitting. This becomes evident if we remind ourselves of the central place given to Holy Scripture in the evangelical Church ever since the days of the Reformation.

The decisive question in Martin Luther's controversy with the papists was this. What must Christians in general, and more specifically teachers of the Church, regard as the source and measuring stick for their doctrinal statements? His opponents endeavored to refute him by arguments taken from the tradition of the fathers and councils. Luther held fast to the principle that Scripture alone was the normative foundation of all preaching and teaching within the Church. Thus the slogan *"sola scriptura"* became the bed rock of evangelical faith and action. The tremendous emphasis on the authority of the Bible is brought out in the Introduction to the Formula of Concord of 1577:

> We believe, teach and confess that the sole rule and measuring stick, according to which all doctrines and teachers are to be judged, are the prophetical apostolic writings of the Old Testament and New Testament only. . . Other writings of ancient and modern teachers, however famous they might be, should not be held equal to Holy Scripture, but should altogether be subjected to it, and should not be accepted otherwise than as witnesses . . .

2

The Reformation believed Scripture to be the only fountain of doctrine. The Bible held the supreme teaching office in the Church. Orthodox Lutherans consequently considered it most important to prove that the Bible, because of its inherent quality, was fully able to exercise its ministry. In refuting the Roman Catholic argument that the Bible was, for laymen, an obscure book full of confusing ambiguity, Lutheran theologians developed a very minute doctrine of the inspiration of the Holy Scripture. As it had come into being, not out of a human decision, but as the Holy Spirit breathed on its human authors, it had necessarily the quality of complete inerrancy, for the Holy Spirit is infallible. This doctrine was applied not only to statements about faith and ethics, but also statements concerning history, chronology, and geography. Some theologians even affirmed that the Bible had been dictated by the Holy Spirit during a complete suspension of the human personality of the writer.

Since Scripture was given to men as the sole and authoritative record of God's saving acts, the Bible was declared to be not only completely reliable but also clear and sufficient for all knowledge necessary for salvation. Thus the statement of the *"claritas et perspicuitas scripturae sacrae"* could be called the central Protestant dogma in theological epistemology.

In order to understand Scripture, it was believed, no supplementary means of interpretation taken from outside are required. Even if the internal evidence of Scripture is not everywhere the same, Scripture is its own and only interpreter. The dark and more difficult passages are to be understood in the light of the plain and clear passages. This procedure would invariably resolve any seeming contradictions which might appear in the different statements of the Bible.

MARXIST INFLUENCE TODAY

If, after this glance into the past, we direct our eyes to the present, the contrast could not be more striking. In Germany today—and in other lands also—there is hardly a faster way to ruin one's reputation as a theologian than to speak of the inspiration of the Bible, its inerrancy, and the absence of self-contradictions. The doctrine of the authority of the Scripture is openly questioned by our younger theological generation and its intellectual leaders. The Church is giving its interest so one-sidedly to social and political involvement that the secular analysis of the world situation seems very much more important than biblical orientation. This fact is seen in many different ways. In one of the preparatory texts for the Fourth General Assembly of the World Council of Churches at Uppsala we read:

> . . . some Christians look upon the processes of secular history as furnishing new divine revelations which the churches must accept: They discern the activity of the Spirit in the emergence of free nations and international solidarities and undertakings where Christians and non-Christians cooperate in seeking justice or peace in the new social structure created by the technological revolution. Such attitudes contest the claim that the Church alone is entrusted with the power to announce the Kingdom of God and that its life and witness is the only true anticipation of the Lord's coming.[1]

More radical in tone but in thorough agreement with the WCC document, a recent conference of young German ministers produced the following statement: "We cannot naively gauge the way we speak and act from the Bible; rather we must seek orientation from contemporary social and personal concerns. In contemporary discussion the Bible meets us as one partner among others."

One wonders how those young theological candidates could arrive at such shocking conclusions! Obviously they reveal acute Marxist influence on their thinking; but this could have happened only because the theological pattern built up during their university studies has suffered severe structural damage. The watering down of their belief in the normativity, reliability, and internal unity of the Bible has been caused by the critical approach and arbitrary reinterpretations of several successive schools of academic "exegesis." We need to look at this more closely.

4

THE HUMAN SIDE OF THE BIBLE

During the Enlightenment of the eighteenth century a great change took place in the theological approach to the Bible. Biblical research came under the powerful influence of modern thinking. Man became conscious of himself within his world and gained great confidence in the ability of his own reason. He developed a new interest in history, understood himself in historical perspective, and evaluated history in the light of his own problems. The new contact with other cultures brought to Western Christendom an insight into other religions. This greatly stimulated the study of comparative religions and the quest for their common content. Scholars no longer looked for biblical texts to prove their dogmatic systems. Rather they sought out the human side of the Bible. Its historic origin received the most attention. The Bible was seen as only one book among others. The analytical and comparative methods of modern literary art were applied to it.

The nineteenth century may be called the classical age of historicism. In it the historical method achieved a dominating role in the interpretation of the Bible. Only this method was regarded as intellectually honest and acceptable. Actually this value judgment prevails even today in university theology. The "historio-critical method" of exegesis was—and is—regarded as scientifically indispensable to any legitimate theological insight. Thus this twisted view of Scripture has actually now assumed the position which, in older Protestant orthodoxy, was occupied by the doctrine of inspiration! Its aim is to secure the intellectual validity of any theological statement basing itself on a biblical text. Thus the famous theologian G. Ebeling calls the development of this method the most important achievement of Protestant theology since the Reformation.[2] He says that the genuine mission of the Reformers can be fulfilled only by the use of the historio-critical method. On the other hand, many Christians believe the method deeply endangers the faith. They regard it as the root of all evil. What is this method exactly?

5

When we use the term "historio-critical method" in the singular, we must realize that it refers to a whole complex of instruments used in the scientific research in the Bible. The collective term "historio-critical method" is somewhat misleading. It has contributed to a false understanding. Some state naively "the consistent application of the historio-critical method is the only adequate way for modern man to reach a genuine understanding of the biblical texts!"

It is important to realize that the hyphenated combination of the two adjectives "historic" and "critical" is not a common practice in other arts and sciences. The term has been specifically coined by a certain school in Protestant theology. The two adjectives express two distinct concerns. A historical interest traces the complicated origins of the biblical books. It asks what situations and traditions have influenced the biblical authors.

A critical interest searches for the authenticity and validity of a particular text as to its form and content.

The historio-critical method is usually divided into three main branches: textual criticism, literary criticism and higher criticism. Textual criticism compares the ancient biblical manuscripts and attempts to establish the probable original wording of the text. Literary criticism tries to establish the literal integrity of a biblical book: is it an inner unity, has it been written by one author only, is it really written by the person to whom it is ascribed? Can we trace a history of oral tradition and revision? What interest can be discovered in such different historical layers? An important part of literary criticism is form criticism which asks, what nature are the different literary units, making up a certain biblical book? They may be historical accounts, hymns, legal documents, creeds, theological discourses.

Finally, higher criticism arises from the fact that certain internal tensions seem to exist between different biblical texts. Two biblical authors or even one may have two sets of different historical data. For example, there are three different accounts of the conversion of Paul

(Acts 9, 22, and 26). Furthermore, theologians feel entitled to establish a certain normative criterion, i.e. a central theological principle within the Scripture from which they evaluate other theological statements in the Bible. For example, is man justified by faith without works, as Paul teaches in Romans, or by works and not by faith alone, as James affirms?

If in the contemporary world with all its theological riddles and paradoxes, we realistically and objectively seek to interpret the Bible in all its inter-relatedness, we should recognize the desirability of approaching biblical texts in a scholarly way. The faith of the Christian community has always been enriched by scholarly research. The biblical accounts of creation, crucifixion, and resurrection are written not to satisfy the demands and interests of historical science. Rather they witness to experiences with God which God's people of the Old and New Testaments have had and which constituted and shaped their faith in Him and His revelation.

The discovery of the historicity of the Bible is a truly liberating experience for us. It shows us that the Bible does not want to be treated as a textbook with inflexible rules and doctrines. Rather it sets forth the manifold offer of God's grace and His calling of each new generation to obedience while still remaining faithful to His promises and commandments. The inflexible dictation theory of inspiration prevented people from understanding the unfolding of God's revelation in history as well as the living humanity of the writers and the active share which (by way of faithful response) they themselves took in formulating their messages.

THE HISTORIO-CRITICAL METHOD GONE BAD

Granting all this, we must not overlook the fact that a historio-critical examination of the Bible entails tremendous dangers. These rise from the fact, of which many theologians are not aware, that no science or art can work absolutely objectively and without any presuppositions. On the contrary, both the selection and the evaluation of the methods of study—and thus also its results—are predetermined to a point by the position which

7

the observer himself has chosen. This principle applies in different degrees to the various branches of arts and sciences. But the complementary theory of the Danish physicist Niels Bahr has shown, that even exact science in its exploration and description of the same natural phenomenon may arrive at different and contradictory statements depending on the perspective of the scientist. Thus the beam of light can be understood both as immaterial wave and also as a close succession of the smallest units of a light "substance."

As theologians we must confess with shame that the scientists have surpassed us in their critical estimate of the presuppositions of their epistemological principles. Many a time the working methods of historio-critical research have been secretly determined by an unreflecting and unwarranted belief in the absoluteness of its concept of reality and its ways of obtaining knowledge. All this has constituted nothing more than a pseudo-scientific justification of a certain philosophical position. By it theologians often fatally blocked the true way of gaining true theological insight.

THREE FATAL PRESUPPOSITIONS

Basically we can discern three fatal presuppositions by which representatives of the historio-critical method have abandoned and are abandoning the basis for fruitful and legitimate research into Scripture. None of these presuppositions is demanded either by Scripture itself or by a true scientific epistemology.

The first presupposition links up with the theological method of attaining insight to epistemological theory developed by the philosophers Descartes (1536-1650) and Kant (1724-1804). They have been explicitly applied to theology by Ernst Troeltsch (1865-1923).[3] This theory of attaining knowledge places at its center "man as subject" who faces that which he wants to know as his object. But it is not possible for man to gain absolute insight into the thing he wants to know. He is limited by the categories of knowledge inherent to his human nature. Thus he can only attain insights into things as they appear to him.

In the existentialist school of Rudolph Bultmann this

idea of the limitation of acquiring knowledge by the perceptibility of man occupies a central place. Here it is maintained that by revelation we cannot receive objective knowledge of metaphysical objects like heaven or life after death. Only those experiences which touch me deeply in the center of my personality are relevant.

Another aspect of this adherence to a general empirical theory of knowledge is that the student of the Bible must accept the closed system of the scientific world-view. Each event is seen as caused by an impulse in accordance to scientific law. Theologians often overlook the fact that modern science no longer attempts to subject the totality of reality to such a closed system. They admit we are not really sure that all processes in nature are determined by unchangeable laws. But curiously, by an act of voluntary subjection to an outdated pseudo-scientific world view, modernist theologians demand that all biblical miracles are to be judged according to the closed system understanding of nature. They apply this norm to everything in the Bible from the creation account to the prediction of Christ's bodily return. It is obvious that, under such circumstances, the historio-critical approach can end up in a wholesale elimination of biblical affirmations. In his famous demythologization program of 1941, Bultmann has catalogued them under the label, "discarded."

The second dangerous presupposition is the conviction of many representatives of the historio-critical method, that understanding a certain biblical author or text basically consists in discovering its individual peculiarity over against all other authors and traditions. Thus the essence is sought in a nominalistic way in the isolated individual. By this process the common nature of all biblical texts is frequently overlooked. Many historio-critical scholars, applying their radical methods of form criticism and higher criticism, have gone so far that they have split the Old Testament and the New Testament into smaller and smaller units which sometimes consist of only half a verse!

In the process of studying these particularities the scholar finally discovers so many seeming contradictions in the texts, that he finally loses his sense of the organic wholeness of the Bible. Thus in many quarters it has become impossible to speak of a common theology of the Old Testament or of the New Testament, and even more impossible to speak of a theology of the whole Bible.

Instead, "biblical theology" has been dissolved in a vast number of theologies or personal concepts, opinions, or conscious reinterpretations by individual authors. By the mutual exclusiveness of their several concepts, all these authors seem to question and criticize each other. Bible readers who follow such "theologians" lose any sense of the authority or even normativity of the Scriptures. Carrying this line of thinking to its logical conclusion Ernst Kaesemann says: "The New Testament is in a shocking degree non-authentic, full of fictions and contradictions."[2]

Such chaotic results of the historio-critical method cannot satisfy these modernist theologians. They seek for an integrating principle which can serve as a center or as a norm of theological evaluation for all the seemingly heterogenous texts. They introduce a distinction between the actual wording of the biblical texts and their real intention. While the wording is conditioned by the historical circumstances and thus transitory, the intention, it is claimed, is of abiding value.

But here we meet the third most dangerous presupposition introduced by representatives of the historio-critical theology: the intention of the texts is "discovered" by way of abstraction from their real words and by means of a guiding question or principle not gained from the texts themselves.

Such a hermeneutical principle is taken from the interpreter's own philosophical predilection and forced upon the biblical text from outside. The modern theologian would not admit this, though it is true. Rather he would point to many biblical texts which (by means of his hermeneutical approach) start radiating truth before our eyes in an amazing fashion. The hermeneutical principle each man uses seems at first glance to produce exactly those relevant answers to our contemporary problems which we had been searching for. But as one looks a bit more thoroughly at the quoted texts and starts exegeting them in their original setting, he will soon discover that no genuine exegesis is offered to us but rather an ingenious, but alien, reinterpretation.

Such an integrating hermeneutical principle was introduced by Bultmann and his school in form of the existential interpretation. Bultmannians ask in what way the intention of a certain text was to change the understanding man had about himself. In describing such human self-understanding, Bultmann to a large degree makes use of the existential analysis which had been developed by the modern philosophy of existence of young Heidegger. It had become widely popularized in Europe by existentialist novels and dramas of modern writers like Camus and Sartre. Bultmann himself believed that this idea of a basic change in man's understanding of himself was in fact the very center of the message of both Paul and Martin Luther. Thus he claimed he had restored the authority of the theology of the reformers over against its idealistic perversion by theological liberals at the end of the last century.

This actually was the reason for the amazing influence of his theology: it appeared to be modern and still genuinely Lutheran at the same time! But his existentialist concept of justification by faith differs substantially from Paul's doctrine of justification. According to Bultmann, man (after the change in his understanding about himself) actually remains alone in his world. The newly gained "openness to the future" appears as a rather vague and impersonal feeling. In the New Testament, however, justification by faith constitutes a new personal fellowship with a living God in Jesus Christ. Bultmann expressly declares this fellowship to be mythological.

THE THEOLOGY OF REVOLUTION

Bultmann's hermeneutical principle was time-bound, however. This is clearly seen by the historical fate into which it is drawn today. Avantgarde German scholars are now firmly committed to leave behind the age of a pessimistic existentialist individualism. They have entered into a new epoch where mankind in its wholeness makes strong efforts to reshape the structures of a socio-economic and political world order. Little attention is paid to the individual and his understanding of his existence. Contemporary interest focuses on the words "history," "social structures," and on "ideologized utopias." These determine

11

men's political action. Thus in our generation the existentialist school has given way to the new theology of revolution.

Christians who used to be opposed to "modern" theology should be careful not to rejoice at this change. There is no reason for optimism. For the basic method of interpretation is the same in both schools. They are both recklessly using the results of radical literary and higher criticism. Both are using the alleged pluralism of the biblical texts in order to introduce their own philosophical key constructing their own hermeneutical systems on the basis of a few arbitrarily selected and reinterpreted texts. Both existentialist and revolutionary theologies are inclined to silence the real message of the documents of biblical revelation. Both do a superb job of proof-texting. The exegesis of both is highly colored by self-interest.

Yesterday an existentialist chamber orchestra played variations of one single theme, the call to make a decision for a personal new understanding of oneself. Today a band of trumpets led by the Old Testament prophets sounds an "ultimate challenge" to the whole church to participate in world revolution, thus bringing the Kingdom of God into this world.

The average congregation, however, finds itself unable, either in the charming tunes of the chamber concert or in the deafening sounds of the trumpets to recognize the voice of its Good Shepherd. It faces the torn document of its traditional faith which looks like a battlefield in which bombs and shells have gouged deep trenches.

A NEW SPIRITUAL APPROACH

It is not my intention merely to unveil the shocking picture of the desolate theological scenery we find in German theology today. One must go on to explore the ultimate consequences of such exegetical methods.

I would also plead for a new understanding of the Bible which relies completely in the interpreting power of the Holy Spirit. It is necessary to do away with an approach to the Bible which sees in it nothing else but a literary collection of contradictory bits of documents, reflecting merely the existential self-understanding or the political utopias of past generations in remote cultural surroundings.

Today's challenge is to rediscover the Bible as (1) the normative embodiment of the revelatory words and acts of God with His elected people in the history of salvation and (2) as the witness of the people's exemplary response in faith or of their regrettable response in disobedience. We are called upon to take up our Bible not to do socioreligious studies, but to ask the Lord to speak His living word through it directly to us. In the same ways He spoke to the prophets, evangelists, and apostles, God speaks to us. He is still able and willing to shepherd, console, exhort, and warn our present generation.

It is most necessary to liberate ourselves from the dictatorship of theological scholars who declare their allegedly scientific approach to be the only possible one to attain to a true understanding of the Bible. Protestant churches recognize no papal office. Nevertheless we are in danger of coming under the control of a multitude of "popes" who are contradicting and superceding each other. I refer to theologians who are imperiously absolutizing their academic methods. Although their views are always hypothetical and opposed by their colleagues or successors, they offer them as indisputable results of scientific research. They declare them normative for all honest Christian faith which wants to cleave to the truth.

Not all modern theologians speak this way, but they do exist. Their ambition to be the teachers of the Church is unbendable. They produce around themselves an atmosphere either of fascination or of intellectual terror. Nobody dares to break this spell. Nobody wants to risk his reputation as an enlightened contemporary or as a respectable modern theologian.

In my own personal experience and by contact with students, I have discovered what a detrimental spell can originate from such pressured belief in "the latest theological science." Thus I never tire of explaining to my students that there is nothing less scientific than to declare things to be "scientifically established." I find my explanation is almost a kind of exorcism under modern circumstances. It has a wonderful liberating effect on the depressed mind.

Those young theologians, depressed by the latest persuasive hermeneutical system, who have lost their sense

13

of humor, are overwhelmed with the joy of the spiritual life which a reopened Bible has given them. They are able to pray again. In Scripture they hear the voice of the living Lord. They experience personal fellowship with Him, who has spiritually and bodily really risen from the dead. They realize that neither His death nor an outdated scientific dogma can keep Him in the grave or evaporate Him into an idea or an example which might possibly be of some influence today.

THE HOLY SPIRIT AND HERMENEUTICS

I have already anticipated the positive step which must follow the refutation of a philosophical pre-conditioned hermeneutical approach in modern academic exegesis. We could call that negative first step the "demythologization of demythologization."

Those modernist theologians who introduce their own philosophical principles of understanding into their methods of exegesis have made one correct observation: there is no understanding of the Holy Scripture without presuppositions. We all need a hermeneutical key which gives us access to a consistent understanding. True, historical approaches to biblical texts might, to a certain degree, clarify the external circumstances under which a biblical book has been written. But they can never give us access to inner understanding. Nobody is touched or overwhelmed by having identified the literary species or historical setting of a biblical text. No preacher thus receives a striking message for his sermon. Rather the decisive act of understanding takes place at the moment that authority which is speaking in and through the text meets something within me which is already predisposed to be spoken to by this authority.

In the same way an unmusical scholar may be able to compile some bibliographical or statistical data from the history of music. But he will never be able to enjoy an oratorio or even to understand it. This also explains why true believers often feel untouched when they listen to a modernist sermon. Possibly the preacher himself did not experience that essential inner understanding! Thus he does not transmit on the wave length the congregation is tuned to. Hear the word in John 10: "My sheep listen to My call; I know them and they follow Me . . . They will not follow a stranger but will run away from him, because they do not recognize the voice of strangers." We have to add, however, that the communications gap can also originate with those who listen to the sermon, if they are not genuine sheep of Christ!

Communication between the Bible and the congregation is made possible by the fact that both are created by the same divine energy, the power of the Holy Spirit. He fills them as a living divine personality. Just as the congregation is the temple of the Holy Spirit thus (according to II Timothy 3:16) the Scripture is called *"theopneustos"* or "blown through by the divine Spirit." The Greek word *"theopneustia"* is translated into Latin by the term *"inspiratio."* It means exactly the same, that the Scripture is blown through by the Holy Spirit. This means that the future advance or the downfall of our churches is dependent on our readiness to say a clear "yes" to the inspiration of the Scripture. Only in this way will our minds regain that unity and authority lost to us by our misdirected hermeneutical approaches.

THE DECISIVE TASK

By this I do not mean that we can return to the doctrine of inspiration developed by Protestant theology not yet aware of the historicity of the biblical books. But I maintain that the demand for a new acceptance of the inspiration of the Bible is placing a decisive task before the entire field of theology in the immediate future. That task is to relate the genuine result of literary research to the authoritative claim of the Holy Scripture to be the essential literary embodiment of God's self-revelation in history. If theology should prove unable to solve this task, it would have ceased rightly to be called theology. It is no longer scholarly occupation with the Logos, *tou theou.* It would then by its own efforts, have eliminated itself as superfluous and irrelevant.

The resolution of those young German ministers, quoted in the beginning, is no mere slip of the tongue. It is the inevitable consequence of a line of approach to which they were introduced by their theological teachers. Thus it is a "mene tekel upharsim" for much modern theology.

Scientific literary research into the historic origins of the Bible can be good and useful, but only as long as we remain aware that the originator of the biblical texts is the Holy Spirit. It was He who gave us this text in its final normative shape in the canon of the Old Testament and New Testament, conceived and accepted by the early Church. The Holy Spirit has given the impulse to all who have been engaged in conceiving, keeping, copying, compiling, and revising the biblical texts. He also preserved them from distortions and false additions. Thus, in the word which has been received and written down by mortal men, we encounter the living voice of God—sometimes directly, sometimes in a manner more obscure to our present understanding. God's word does not need to be rewritten or reshaped in every cultural change. It does not need to be reinterpreted by any philosophical principles. God's word is able to speak to us in our space age as directly as it did to the Greeks in the first century and to the Papuans in their Stone Age culture at the beginning of this century.

Sometimes we meet people who try to discredit the method of making direct use of a biblical text by asking such vexing questions as "what does this mean today?" or "how can we speak about God today?" These questions are based on wrong presuppositions. But they do point us, against their own intention, toward a correct observation. True understanding presupposes an inner likeness of that which is to be understood and of him who wants to understand. The hermeneutic of modernist theology tries to accomplish this task by reformulating the text in philosophical or sociological terms taken from our situation, but leading to falsification and even to an offence against God's majesty!

That which needs to be changed is not the text but rather the inner attitude of men which causes their difficulty in understanding. God himself offers to make this change in us. It can take place when the Holy Spirit himself takes possession of us from within, makes us receptive to God's voice, regenerates and illuminates our distorted reason, and transforms us into the image of His Son. All those who have received the offer of salvation in Jesus Christ,

16

have by faith and baptism also received the Spirit of sonship. It is this Spirit of Christ within us who in hearing the word of the Bible, hears and recognizes His own word.

The person who has not received the Spirit of sonship is according to the words of Paul still a "natural man." To him the judgment applies: "The unspiritual man does not receive the things of the Spirit of God, for they are folly to him, and he is not able to understand them because they are spiritually discerned." The Christian, however, is entitled to confess: "We have received, not the spirit of the world, but the Spirit that comes from God, in order that we may know the things which God has freely given us."

Now the relationship between the spiritual and the natural man is not one of sociologically separated groups. Even when Christians rely on their own natural reason, they have left the spiritual realm and have become natural men again. Even the Christian theologian can gain a genuine insight into the Bible only to the degree in which he approaches the Scripture in the Spirit and in the obedience of faith.

MODERNIST MISERY

The misery of modernist theology is that it has participated in the original sin of the Enlightenment, the idolization of man's reason. In a hidden way idolization of our unilluminated reason is still influencing all our theological work, even the work of many conservative scholars.

The healing of our theology and our churches in Europe and America can only take place if we penitently subject our intellect in faith to the guidance of the Holy Spirit. This guidance can be gained only by a personal life in the Spirit and by listening to the continuous self explication of the divine Word within the fellowship of the Church of Jesus Christ. Theologians can never claim to be teachers of the Church as long as they act as autonomous interpreters of the Bible who respect only the thorough application of their "scientific" methods. They can become valid teachers of the Church only to the degree they enter the field where the Holy Spirit is displaying His energies. This means at the same time that they carefully study the living history of biblical interpretation which is the special

17

field of the Holy Spirit's work. They must humbly join the chain of witnesses, not so much as historical critics, but rather as the faithful stewards of God's mysteries.

What taking these insights seriously will mean to traditional academic theology can hardly be described. The revolutionary consequences will be tremendous. As one of my friends prophetically remarked: "We are approaching the time for an exodus out of all familiar ecclesiastical and theological patterns, the dimension of which can hardly be conceived. We shall be thrown back upon the basic elements of our Christian life. We shall have to learn again how to express our faith. A complete and thoroughly biblical restructuring of our theological way of thinking is coming."

At a time when everyone is talking about new structures, we recognize the need for new structures breathed on by the Holy Spirit and controlled by Scripture properly understood. These are really fundamental to a true renewal of our churches and missions.

2

The Struggle for
Spiritual Identity

In his annual report to the General Assembly of the
Evangelical (i.e., Protestant) Church in Germany in January, 1971, the presiding bishop, Hermann Dietzfelbinger,
shocked delegates with the following statement:

> If I am not totally deceived, we are right in the middle
> of a struggle for the faith, of a Kirchenkampf com-
> pared to which the Kirchenkampf under the Nazis was
> only a skirmish. The frightening aspects of it are that
> hardly anyone is aware of it, that it is generally played
> down, and that it is making headway under the mis-
> leading terms like "pluralism!" [1]

A few weeks later the titular leader of Germany's
Protestants sharpened his remarks at a meeting in Brun-
swick. He called for the urgent convocation of a "confessional" synod. This reminded his audience of the historic
Confessional Synod of Barmen that was launched by the
anti-Nazi Confessing Church in 1934.

These declarations caused a commotion in churches all
over Germany. They were welcomed by the "confessing"
groups, which had been trying to say the same thing for
the last five years. Others rejected them entirely or played
them down as an overstatement. They claimed that the
conflict was a matter of semantics rather than of faith.

Germany's leading Protestant journal, *Evangelische Kommentare*, for example, commented editorially on Dietzfelbinger's statement under the title "False Alarm."

This theological conflict in Germany is serious enough to attract the attention of fellow Christians in other countries. Although it concerns theological trends in general, the reader will see immediately that it goes directly to the heart of vital missiological concern. In this chapter, I shall attempt to give a clear outline of the situation. I make no pretense of doing so from a neutral position. In spiritual matters, neutrality is always illegitimate. I speak as a representative of those who have taken a definite stand for biblical, confessing Christianity.

THEOLOGICAL CHANGE IN THE FIFTIES

When I began my theological studies soon after World War II, the Confessing Church had just triumphed over the party of the so-called German Christians who, with Hitler's support, had controlled both the theological seminaries and the church councils. The Confessing Church was strongly influenced by the dialectical theology of Karl Barth, tempered with a strong emphasis on the two great reformers, Luther and Calvin. The salvation-history approach to the Bible pioneered by Oscar Cullman and Gerhard von Rad was coming into its own.

Theological study during these years of hope for spiritual renewal as seen over against our national collapse was a thrilling experience. Despite a moderately critical approach to the Bible, our professors imparted a basically positive attitude toward the authority and relevance of the scriptural revelation and the history of Christian teaching. There was no doubt that God's self-disclosure and His redeeming work in the death and resurrection of Jesus Christ formed the basic content and norm of the Church's ministry. We did not hesitate to take our stand within the Church of Jesus Christ. We knew that a spiritual renewal within the Church was the first condition for witnessing for Him in the world.

The first nation-wide "Kirchentag" of German Protestants was held in 1949. Others followed at two-year intervals.

They were great celebrations of faith. They demonstrated the solidarity of the Christian community in East and West Germany and attracted hundreds of thousands of people. Bible studies led by noted spiritual leaders were the most popular item on the varied program of the rallies.

Youth and student work were flourishing as well. I can still remember how we packed the lecture halls in Halle and Heidelberg to hear our university chaplains and theological professors lead weekly Bible studies. A kind of biblical renewal blew like a refreshing breeze through our churches and seminaries. Later, on the mission field, I observed that the most dedicated German missionaries were often those who had been called during those seven years immediately after World War II.

However, by the end of that period we could detect a wind of change. There was a notable relationship between this and our German economic recovery. The spiritual seriousness that marked the war generation was less evident among younger persons, who were enjoying an easier and more affluent life. The quest for intellectual truth for its own sake began to take the upper hand, displacing the hunger for spiritual nurture and the desire for maturity.

BULTMANN'S STAR RISES

At that juncture one theologian above others burst into prominence. He was not a youngster. He was a contemporary of Karl Barth. Together with Emil Brunner and Friedrich Gogarten, he had helped Barth launch "dialectical theology" during the 1920's. His name was Rudolf Bultmann. The moment had come for him to carry out a program called the "demythologizing" of the New Testament.

In 1951 Bultmann republished his 1941 manifesto, "New Testament and Mythology," in a series of essays called *Kerygma and Mythos.* [2] This launched a tremendous public debate. Bultmann contended that the New Testament frequently uses the mythological language of the first-century world to express non-mythical revealed truth. This truth is essentially concerned not with cosmology or historical events but with an existential transformation of man's self-understanding, his concept of the meaning of life,

21

and his attitude toward his neighbor. To bring out the real significance of the New Testament for modern man, we have to free the essential Gospel message from the non-essential mythical framework and translate it into a more appropriate terminology. This terminology Bultmann borrowed from the existentialist philosopher, Martin Heidegger.

This program of demythologization, it is true, was not originally meant to eliminate biblical truth. It was supposed to be a contemporary translation. The translation was achieved, however, at a tremendous cost in biblical substance. Let me quote from "New Testament and Mythology":

> Man's knowledge and mastery of the world have advanced to such an extent through science and technology that it is no longer possible for anyone seriously to hold the New Testament view of the world . . .And if this is so, we can no longer accept the story of Christ's descent into hell or his ascension into heaven as literally true. We can no longer look for the return of the Son of Man on the clouds of heaven or hope that the faithful will meet him in the air (I Thess. 4:15ff.). Now that the forces and laws of nature have been discovered, we can no longer believe in spirits, whether good or evil . . . The miracles of the New Testament have ceased to be miraculous . . . It is impossible to use electric light and the wireless . . . and at the same time to believe in the New Testament world of demons and spirits . . . The mythical eschatology is untenable for the simple reason that the parousia of Christ never took place as the New Testament expected. History did not come to an end and, as every schoolboy knows, it will continue to run its course. [3]

When in 1951 Bultmann made these pronouncements before the whole Protestant Church in Germany, it caused a considerable reaction. Many individual theologians and clergymen alerted the general Christian public. They demanded that the churches condemn Bultmann's doctrine. Some church councils and synods actually took up the issue, and a condemnation appeared imminent. However, other theologians and churchmen such as Martin Niemoller and Werner Ehlert rushed to Bultmann's defense. As a result, apart from some pastoral letters warning against dangerous theological tendencies, no disciplinary action was taken. Instead, the mass media picked up the debate and stimulated even more interest. In subsequent years more and more professorships in New Testament exegesis were awarded to Bultmann's disciples. The existentialist school, under its euphemistic name "kerygmatic theology," predominated not only in New Testament studies, but also in systematic and practical theology.

The results of this theological shift during the 50's cannot be overestimated. It created an entirely new atmosphere in the seminaries. It produced a new type of theological student who joylessly brooded over his existentialist self-understanding. Soon Bultmann's influence began to be felt in the congregations, where his ideas were expounded from the pulpit. In the schools, religious instruction was turned into a reinterpretation of biblical writings according to the new theory. Before long, Bultmannite ministers were promoted to responsible positions in church administration.

Even more significantly, this new hypercritical school of biblical interpretation developed a missionary-like zeal to enlighten the whole church. Cheap pamphlets appeared to popularize the alleged results of so-called scientific theology. The churches were criticized for not changing sooner and for keeping their people in ignorance for so long. The mass media, including the big magazines, radio, and television, gleefully pounced upon these sensational "discoveries" and secured for them the widest possible publicity. One of the most disastrous developments was the capture of all key positions in the religious communications service by these "modern" theologians. Quite often these were men whose personal faith had been destroyed in seminary and who therefore felt unfit to become pastors.

In 1966, the modernist takeover of the seminaries and churches was almost complete. Something had to be done. A group of orthodox or pietistic theologians and pastors decided to join together to form the "No Other Gospel" movement, also called the "Confessional Movement." Theological leadership was provided by Walter Kunneth,

23

professor of systematic theology in Erlangen. Kunneth had been one of the fiercest opponents of Hitler's ideology of "blood and toil."

As it turned out, however, by the time the Confessional Movement was organized, the severest attacks against the historic faith were no longer coming from the ranks of Bultmann's school. A new force, the revolutionary movement, was taking its place.

THE REVOLUTIONARY MOVEMENT

Compared with the situation of the earlier sixties that produced the Confessional Movement, the ecclesiastical and theological picture has changed. It has not reverted to the spiritual conditions of the postwar period. We have not yet experienced either a renewal of classical Lutheran orthodoxy or a large-scale spiritual revival of evangelical piety. Some hopeful signs have only begun to appear in recent months.

The most staggering change has come through a great mass movement, ignited not by any outstanding academic theologian, but by the world-wide chain reaction of the student revolution. Its chief ideologists were not theologians but Neo-Marxist philosophers and sociologists, such as Herbert Marcuse and Ernst Bloch. When the international wave of student revolt swept the theological seminaries and the Christian university groups, the soil had, however, already been prepared by some theological developments.

Radical biblical criticism, first of all, had produced a large-scale sellout of biblical authority and confessional orthodoxy. For several years such criticism was considered the "in thing" of theological study. Lectures on it attracted the largest student enrollments. But suddenly the students seemed to become aware that what they had been doing was undermining the substance of the biblical revelation itself, from which they were supposed to live and upon which they were to draw as ministers. In the name of "kerygmatic theology," the basic elements of the biblical kerygma had been disintegrated.

The final consequence had been drawn by Herbert Braun, Bultmann's most radical disciple. Braun claimed that God Himself is not an objective personality or entity existing independently from the universe He has created. Instead, Braun conceived of Him as a certain form of human inter-relatedness. He is the "thou shalt" and the "thou mayest," the "source of my drivenness." That is to say, "God" becomes merely a conventional expression to signify a hidden, vital impulse to live courageously and responsibly. This word does not give us any definite content related to our prospects for the future, nor does it supply any norms for our ethical behavior. It simply urges us to live in neighborly fashion according to the challenge of a changing situation.

THE MISERY OF CHRISTIANITY

One of the most brilliant theological students of this period, Joachim Kahl, who had himself just gone through this educational process and taken his doctorate in Marburg, wrote a book that became a bestseller among theological students for a whole year. It caused many to give up theology entirely. Its title was *The Misery of Christianity: A Plea for Humanism Without God*. Kahl presented a synopsis of mutually-contradictory statements of contemporary theologians, unmasked the hollowness of many clichés of this theology and concluded that chaos existed in exegesis, dogmatics, and ethics. Remarkably enough, although Kahl himself is an agnostic, his chief target was not the remains of orthodoxy but the kerygmatic school. He called demythologization "a manipulation of authoritative texts for current use" and "organized dishonesty and ambiguity." [4]

Although many theological students were impressed by Joachim Kahl, not all of them followed his example by leaving both their vocation and the church. During the student riots in 1968 and 1969, attempts were made to forge a new concept, not only of theology but of the entire function of the Christian Church.

To some extent these efforts attempted to elaborate theological ideas that had already appeared during the Bultmannite era. An example would be Bonhoeffer's theses: that humanity has come of age, that we are at the end of the religious era, and that the task of the Church is to follow the example of Jesus as "the man for others." We might also mention two new hypotheses for a theology

25

of history. First, Wolfhart Pannenberg's Hegelian-inspired concept of world history as revelation, and secondly Jurgen Moltmann's "theology of hope," which owes at least as much to the "principle of hope" of Marxist philosopher Ernst Bloch as it does to biblical prophecies of the coming Kingdom.

Even more important was the theology of secularization conceived by Friedrich Gogarten and taken up by Arend van Leeuwen, Harvey Cox, and J.C. Hoekendijk. Through Hoekendijk and Walter Hollenweger this theology of secularization became the accredited ideology of the World Council of Churches. It reached a new peak of influence at the WCC's Geneva Conference in 1966 and at the Uppsala Assembly in 1968. This whole series of concepts, different as they might be in emphasis, started from a mild humanism and ended up with a definition of revolution as participation in God's activities in history. It has in common the assertion that the Church does not exist for its own sake, nor for the sake of a transcendental, personal God, but for the world. Its main purpose is to humanize society by changing political and social structures. This purpose can be achieved only if the church is radically changed. Its structures must be secularized so that it can become more directly involved in the affairs of the world.

A still more radical contingent of young theologians did not even try to preserve Christian appearances. They openly dedicated themselves to plain Marxism in its anarchistic, Leninistic, and Maoist brands. For them no theology was adequate to produce what was most needed, the revolution. If some of these continued as theologians or even became ministers, they did so for two reasons. First, they thought it was necessary to study theology in order to overcome it. From the inside they could unmask its ideological function in the history of Christian society. Here the radical criticism of religion and Christianity expounded by Feuerbach, Marx, Nietzsche, Freud, and others was welcomed. Students even promoted counter-evangelism, attempting to convert their fellow-students from their former religious outlook to a supposedly more scientific, utopian sociological outlook.

The second reason some continued in the ministry was tactical. Since the majority of church members still had some sentimental religious concepts and desires, these radical young theologians thought they had to be ministers in order to deal with them. Moreover, in order to capture the machinery of the church and to transform it into an instrument of social change, the revolutionaries had to work from within. Their ultimate purpose, however, was to destroy old institutions such as churches and seminaries and to replace them with the new structures designed for revolutionary action.

Once this movement started, Germany experienced two years of outrageous and even blasphemous performances. Prayer was abandoned, worship services and other church meetings were disrupted, and finally the "theologians" themselves were distributing leaflets and putting up posters that ridiculed all the basic Christian doctrines. Theological students at Münster even staged a Black Mass dedicated to Satan!

More recently these groups have become less outrageous in their behavior. This does not reflect a real change in conviction, as much as the adoption of a more careful, long-range strategy. Personally, I am more concerned about the groups that still take an interest in theology. Here we meet professors who in effect adapt traditional Christian concepts to the expectations and wishes of the new generation. They use language that appears quite traditional, and that sounds in fact increasingly orthodox. But its content becomes ever more humanistic and this-worldly. What is euphemistically called "socially relevant" or "political" theology is really a camouflaged atheistic humanism.

THE PROMISE OF THE SERPENT

In his book *Atheism in the Bible,* Ernst Bloch expounds the thesis that the secret theme of the Bible is the promise of the serpent in the Garden of Eden: "Ye shall be like God." This prophecy, Bloch says, has been fulfilled by Jesus Christ. When Jesus said, "I and the Father are one," He actually dethroned the sovereign God and installed himself, as a man, in God's dignity. A group of participants in a missions seminar in Hamburg came to the following conclusion:

> The traditional statements about the return of Christ,
> that God will be all in all, etc., aim functionally
> at man's becoming man, a goal to which Christian
> mission is calling and paving the way, but which is
> not given to man to reach on his own. [5]

We may rightly say that the "death-of-God" theology was of only passing significance. Today, however, it is being replaced by the "man-is-God" theology, which is actually the theology of the Antichrist. This theology is being exported to Asian and African churches by, for example, the Ecumenical Institute of Chicago. It is important to recognize that this whole development has been made possible by what that institution calls "the revolution in theology." They really mean by this the destruction of faith in biblical revelation by the consistent application of higher criticism to the biblical texts.

CONFESSING EVANGELICAL CHRISTIANITY

One of the most disastrous aspects of the present crisis of faith in Germany is the inability of the official church to inform its members clearly as to which doctrines and practices are consistent with its confessional commitment and to discipline those who persist in violating that commitment.

There are two reasons for this paralysis of the church. One is the pluralism within the theological seminaries, which for centuries had been considered the touchstones in doctrinal matters. The other reason is the growing polarization between church workers. Both "conservatives" and "progressives" insist that their view must become the official one of the whole church. As a result, any authoritative pronouncement on doctrinal or ethical matters is sure to be opposed by one section of the church or another. There are very few church leaders of the caliber of Bishop Dietzfelbinger who would dare defend the standards of the church in public. One of the most despicable aspects of the situation is the fact that, as we have noted, most key positions in the Christian press are held by modernists who constantly publish distorted reports and highly biased comments. They suppress news of conservative groups,

28

including their public statements. In church elections, they engage in extensive propagandizing of the voters. Their publications receive large subsidies from official church revenues, whereas no conservative publication would have the slightest chance of receiving subsidies. There is little hope that a Christian periodical comparable in doctrinal position, size and intellectual level with *Christianity Today* could be established in Germany.

Here is where the new Confessional Movement comes in. It defends biblical standards of doctrine and ethics and their validity in the church, in missions, and for society in general. It has to act in place of the official teaching authorities of the church and build up a parallel communications network. Actually the Confessional Movement is a whole complex of analogous groups that sprang up independently of one another. All reacted to the takeover of modern theology in the fifties and to the infiltration of radical leftists into the Church and its institutions. The oldest of these grew out of Wurttemberger pietism. Labeled the Ludwig Hofacker Conference, it was established in 1951. The largest group, which soon took over the leadership of the protest was the "No Other Gospel" or Confessional Movement. It was launched in March, 1966, with a mass rally in Dortmund's Westfalenhalle. It drew from Westphalian and Rhenish pietism, but it was also inspired by the Reformation and by the *Kirchenkampf* against the Nazis. Another branch of the Confessional Movement, the "Church Rally *(Kirchliche Sammlung)* for Bible and Confession," was also founded in 1966. Distinctively a Lutheran confessional group, it maintained close relationships with similar groups in Scandinavia. Sister movements were founded during the following years in Bavaria and Berlin.

All these movements are made up primarily of lay and ordained members of the established Protestant churches. They make their appeal to the church administration and to the existing congregations. At this time, they do not seek separation from the established churches. Their goal is rather a doctrinal and spiritual renewal within the churches. Thus they take every opportunity for responsible consultation with church leaders and with the older, established missionary societies. They seek to play the role of a "loyal opposition" within their denominations.

Since 1969 these groups have tended to work in ever closer cooperation. In 1969 the "Theological Assembly" *(Theologischer Konvent)* was founded in Frankfurt with Professor Walter Kunneth as president. It united prominent theologians in an attempt to give theological leadership in the spiritual confusion of our time. It might be called the brain trust of the Confessional Movement.

One opportunity for joint witness was the 1969 *Kirchentag* in Stuttgart. The *Kirchentag* planners wanted to limit its scope to social and political issues. But the Confessional Movement refused to participate unless one section of the *Kirchentag* addressed itself to the burning doctrinal issue. Thus Section I assembled under the heading "Conflict About Jesus." Contrary to all expectations, this section proved by far the greatest attraction. For three days the largest hall was jammed to overflowing with 9,000 people as three modernist and three conservative scholars confronted one another in a debate about the divine nature and the return of Christ.

In March, 1970, the Theological Assembly came to public attention for the first time by issuing the "Frankfurt Declaration on the Fundamental Crisis of Christian Mission." By October the spirit of solidarity had developed so far that the five conservative groups formed a federation called "The Conference of Confessing Fellowships in the Evangelical Churches in Germany." Its purpose is to provide a united witness in matters concerning all the Protestant churches of Germany, especially their inner life, their mission, and their public responsibility. One of its first tasks was to appeal to the West German government and legislature about proposed revisions to the criminal code on pornography and abortion.

At the moment our Conference is concerned with the attempt to change the federal structures of both the Protestant state churches and the German Protestant Missionary Council into centralized bodies with legislative and executive authority. We are not opposed in principle to closer unity in church and mission. But we are convinced that the projected unity can be achieved only at the price of doctrinal truth. Furthermore, we recognize that the primary motive for merger at this time is basically the desire for a more extensive engagement in social and political issues. It looks toward a further secularization of the Church. It would ultimately be turned into a syncretistic welfare organization in alliance with the powers of this world. Our protest is therefore taken from the watchword of the 1937 Oxford Conference: "Let the Church be the Church."

Some may charge that this is just a specter dreamed up by sectarian minds in order to justify their opposition to ecumenical ventures. But we continually see signs of a fatal change in the way the churches, the missionary societies, and the World Council of Churches see themselves and their role. They think of themselves as instruments to bring about the world society of the future, composed of people of all religions and ideologies.

This new understanding of mission was trumpeted forth in 1971 in a huge publicity campaign. Picture magazines and posters appeared everywhere, portraying a group of armed guerrillas in Africa with the inscription, "Today we are partners . . . Mission today is the mandate given to all Christians to fight together against everything that destroys life, against racism, intolerance, exploitation and alienation . . ." None of these magazines and posters anywhere indicated that mission has primarily to do with preaching the Gospel and with gathering Christ's Church from all nations. Although most of the Christians who actively support missions were disgusted with this advertisement, it was hailed by the Ecumenical Press Service and recommended for imitation by other countries.

EVANGELICAL SOLIDARITY AND RENEWAL

On the other hand, this campaign has inadvertently helped bring about greater solidarity among conservative evangelicals. The "Conference of Evangelical Missionary Societies" decided to adopt the Frankfurt Declaration and to cooperate more closely with the Theological Assembly. This decision brought the Evangelical Alliance and the Conference of Confessional Fellowships into close contact, which means that now the non-state-related Protestant churches in Germany are also joining in the *Kirchenkampf*.

31

An important addition to the strength of the Conference of Confessing Fellowships came in March, 1972. Then the Gnadau Union, the federation of all the pietistic fellowships, institutions, and missions in the state churches, formally adopted the Frankfurt Declaration and joined the conference as its sixth constituent body. This means that the conference's work will become more and more clearly rooted in the evangelical lay membership of the churches, thus balancing out the predominance of clergy in the Church Rally groups.

The role of confessing evangelical Christianity is by no means confined to the apologetic task in our present struggle. "Resistance and renewal" are the two great concerns of the Confessional Movement. Without this second, reviving element, we would be nothing more than a kind of "orthodoxy patrol." The confessing fellowships from the beginning have seen it as their chief task to nourish the spiritually starved masses of evangelical believers, who have often looked in vain for a proclamation of the biblical Gospel in their church services.

This spiritual nurture is provided in various ways. Mass rallies have been an outstanding method. They are not simply old-style revival meetings; they combine a reaffirmation of the confessions, evangelistic proclamation, and solid Christian teaching. A new term has been coined to describe this form of ministry: "teaching evangelization." The biblical doctrine of the person of Christ, His work, His bodily resurrection, the reality of His personal return, and the significance of prayer are important elements of these popular rallies.

Another, more personal approach is found in weekend courses concentrating on Bible study. Suggestions are given for establishing and maintaining small cells in Christian homes, focused on Bible study, intercession, and mutual responsibility.

We also realize that in spite of the necessary new emphasis on the lay structure of the Church, the pastor still holds a key position. Therefore vacation courses for theological students are conducted in an effort to "vaccinate" them against modernist infections and to build up a sound biblical substance for their personal theology. This is also done in the new theological hall established in Tubingen in 1970, named for Albrecht Bengel, a well-known Bible expositor and one of the fathers of Wurttemberg pietism. Here students are formed into a close Christian fraternity and are also brought into vital contact with some of the healthiest parishes in the country.

Two crucial questions might finally be asked: What are the prospects of saving the Church in Germany from spiritual ruin? What are the prospects of a revival of evangelical faith and life? The answers cannot be given with absolute certainty, mainly because we do not know exactly where we are in God's plan of world salvation. If much time still remains to complete the task of proclaiming the Gospel to all nations, we surely may hope and pray for a new spiritual reformation and revival in our German churches. There are some signs that such a revival is beginning, especially among the younger generation. But if we are living shortly before the end times, we may be in for a still greater apostasy and even for persecution. We are trying to prepare the Church for both possibilities. In either case Christ's charge and promise are the same: "Be loyal though it means your death, and I shall give you the crown of life" (Rev. 2:10)

3

Sharpening Definitions in Mission

Now that we have laid a foundation for developing a contemporary theology of mission, we must move on to the task of defining terms. As precise definitions emerge, mission theology will become proportionately clearer.

THE CHURCH FOR OTHERS?

In recent years no one theological description of the Church has seemed to be able to capture the younger generation within the ecumenical movement as much as Bonhoeffer's phrase "the Church for others." This appears to be the concept which can effectively break down the walls of that religious ghetto we so often build up as individuals and as small ecclesiastical groups. It seems to move us along to "where the action is," joining us with those socially-oriented groups which strive for a more human society and a better world. The authors of the study carrying the same title, written in preparation for the Uppsala Assembly of the World Council of Churches in 1969, summarize their underlying motivation as follows:

> Is the church an educational institution for children,
> a pastime for adults, an institution of salvation,
> a place of relaxation, an instrument for preaching

the Word and administering the sacraments, or is the church there for others? The two working groups were searching for a church which is not a stumbling block to itself, in which communion transcends the subcultures, a church which does not only interpret the world but changes it. [1]

I think we should try to listen to the positive aspects of this statement attentively and sympathetically, despite an undercurrent which may remind us more of Karl Marx than of Martin Luther. Certainly the very nature of the Gospel demands that it not be for us Christians a dead end street. Whoever has been redeemed by Christ is at once called to become a witness of this to others. Multitudes of others must also become beneficiaries of Christ's liberating work. No one who has received the slightest touch of the Spirit of Christ can remain indifferent to the frantic attempt of our contemporary world to create conditions for life which are more human. The Christian disciple will share his Lord's reaction: "But as He looked at the multitudes He was filled with pity over them because they were like shepherdless sheep that are wearied and helpless" (Mt. 9:36).

This account of Matthew carries an immensely important lesson. It shows that in order to bring salvation to suffering mankind in today's world, it is not enough simply to react to some of the anxious emergency calls of the world and then to ponder how the Church might join others who are already busy meeting those needs. Some Christians seem to hold a mistaken belief that three things alone are essential to redeem the world: (1) a socio-political analysis of the present situation, (2) a good intention to get as involved as possible, and (3) technical know-how. This is one reason why the most important ecumenical tasks today are referred to so-called expert conferences whose findings then simply are endorsed by more representative bodies or general assemblies..

But let us beware — the world itself does not possess the key that solves its own deepest problems. Even in Jesus' time, many religious and political leaders rendered important services to the people. But realizing all of this, Jesus nevertheless called the crowd a helpless flock of sheep with no shepherd. Nowhere do we find a simplistic appeal to the good will of the disciples to get "involved." Jesus does not attempt to stir them up with analyses, statistics, and programs, spurring them to political or ecclesiastical activism.

JESUS' ANSWER

Jesus' answer for the world's problems was at once more complex and more profound. Four basic features in Matthew 9-10 combine to present a highly relevant message to us.

First, Matthew states that Jesus Himself went about all the cities and villages preaching the Gospel and healing every disease (Mt. 9:35). Notice that the point of departure is His mission, His charity, and above all, His victorious ability to let the Kingdom of God break into this suffering world.

Secondly we see Jesus' compassion, which for the first time uncovers the true need of the world (Mt. 9:36). Still we are astonished at how smoothly the depressing image of the scattered flock is transformed into the joyful vision of a field covered with a plentiful harvest. The needs of this world become the very opportunities for the victory of the Kingdom. This is not to be taken in the Marxist sense that a "conscientization" concerning the injustice of the present social structures is a necessary first step in the dialectical process, and that these structures will inevitably be overthrown. Rather, it means that this suffering world is open for the dynamic invasion of the forces of messianic salvation.

The third feature of our text is consistently the most amazing one to me. While Jesus does not appeal to His disciples to "volunteer for missionary service," He does exhort them to pray the Lord to send laborers into His harvest (Mt. 9:38). In the Greek original a more colorful word is used: *e k b a l l e* which means literally "to fling out." Here at a very decisive juncture we meet the true biblical understanding of vocation. It is something rather different from simply a well-meant resolution. Rather it impresses us with the inscrutability and the unshakable determination of God Himself to elect the people through whom He is going to carry out His plan of salvation.

Finally, the fourth feature of the text is that Jesus Himself selects and ordains His twelve apostles for their ministry (Mt. 10:1-5). He sends them out as His personally authorized representatives to undertake exactly the same saving tasks which He had been performing.

THE MEANING OF MISSION

The meaning of the word "mission" must be thoroughly understood at this point. Mission does not mean to get aligned as partners with the forces of all men of good will who are desirous to help others. Many of these men have mixed motives. Some are power-seekers, and for that or also for ideological motives incompatible with the Gospel, they set themselves to overcome the emergency situation of the world. In mission, however, we deal with the unfathomable mystery that God Himself selects and dignifies a group of people to share in Christ's redemptive work by His divine authority. This insight shows the illegitimacy of many modern concepts of "God's mission" often expressed as "what Christ is doing in the world." These phrases are nothing more than pious descriptions of the attempts of certain secular forces to bring about solutions to certain socio-political problems, combined with the demand that the Church support these attempts. At Uppsala it was maintained that mission, in order to be relevant, must guide itself by the "agenda of the world."

The Willingen Assembly of the International Missionary Council in 1952 maintained a much more genuinely biblical insight concerning the relationship between the Gospel and the claims of the world. It made the following remarkable statement, which apparently was ignored at Uppsala:

> The Cross does not answer the world's questions, because they are not the real questions. It confronts the world with the real questions, which are God's questions—casting down all that exalts itself in defiance of Him, bringing to nothing the idolatries by which men are deceived, and raising up those who are sunk in disillusionment and despair. [2]

If we want fully to understand the nature and claims of our mission, first of all we must understand the nature of Christ's own redemptive mission. Only after having grasped the meaning of His ministry, past, present, and future, can we tackle the matter of what our missionary vocation is all about.

Our mission, in a word, is the continuation of Christ's mission. It is the active participation in the continuing ministry of the risen and reigning Christ. This ministry can only be understood properly as it is seen against the backdrop of the Messianic expectations of the people of the Old Testament. The Old Testament is characterized by significant tensions between its universalistic outlook concerning creation and eschatological redemption on the one hand, and its particularism with regard to revelation and election on the other. But right from the beginning the election of Israel is determined by her calling to fulfill a vicarious mission to the Gentiles. In the introduction to God's revelation on Mount Sinai we find this profound statement: "You will become to Me a kingdom of priests, a holy nation" (Exodus 19:6). But at the same time it is true that nowhere in the history of the old covenant do we find a definite missionary mandate given to Israel. The salvation of all nations, coming from Mount Zion, remains an eschatological vision.

Oscar Cullman suggests one key toward solving this riddle. He speaks of "progressive reduction in the history of salvation." This means that God progressively sharpens the focus of the carrier of this priestly and prophetic commission from the entire people of Israel to the specific tribe of Judah, to the holy remnant, and finally to the person of the suffering servant of God in Isaiah 53. As corporate personality, the servant represents the whole body of the true Israel. In virtue of His suffering, the messianic rule shall ultimately be extended over all nations. "Therefore I will give to Him His portion among the great, and with mighty ones shall He a portion gain. For He poured out His soul unto death . . ." (Isaiah 53:12).

But this song about the suffering servant was not correctly understood by the Jewish people. It is true that when Jesus began His mission, the Jews held various messianic expectations. But the person of the Servant of the Lord did not seem to play a vital part in them.

Right from the beginning Jesus stressed the Kingdom as the focus of His preaching and teaching. He gave clear indications that in His proclamation, through His deeds, and in His very person, the Kingdom of God was already present. "But if I expel demons by means of the finger of God, then the Kingdom of God has already reached you" (Luke 11:20).

As a matter of fact, it did not take long for the Jewish people to begin to associate their messianic expectations with Jesus. According to John 6:15 this happened in connection with His miracle of multiplying the loaves. But events subsequently take a strange turn. In the very moment when Peter, representing the disciples, unveils the messianic secret (Mt. 16:16), Jesus embarks on a different course. He plays down His messianic dignity and begins His last journey to Jerusalem. The three synoptic Gospels agree that Jesus consciously chose the road of suffering, and that He regarded His death as a necessary part of the divine plan of salvation. The first interpretation is found in Mark 10:45 (a passage which historiocriticism has attempted in vain to invalidate) "For even the Son of Man did not come to be served but to serve and to give His life a ransom for many." Here we find a profound implication of Christ's historic mission. The service which He came to render to mankind by virtue of His death is specifically to redeem men and women from their guilt and from their separation from God.

By Christ's vicarious self-sacrifice, the barrier separating Israel from the rest of the nations is removed. While the earthly Jesus of Nazareth followed a mission limited to the lost sheep of Israel, His blood shed for the many becomes the propitiation and the foundation for the reconciliation of all Gentiles as well. The resurrection of Christ then brings His installation into the universal dominion. Now by divine right all nations are His. From now on, history aims at but one goal: the establishment of Christ's rule over all nations. This is to be accomplished by preaching the Gospel everywhere, and baptizing those who are gathered to become His people. These people of

God, in faith and obedience, testify to their Lord and thereby become the salt and light of their particular social environment.

But even this gathering of Christ's eschatological community from among all nations and its subsequent radiation into all the world is still not the final fruit of the ministry of the ascended Christ.

This present age is rather an intermediate time. The *de facto* reign of Christ still seems to be limited or even totally subdued by the power of sin, death, and the devil. The triumph of Christ cannot yet be seen in its universal significance. Neither can it be demonstrated by external means. The reign of Christ still takes the form of service, in which His followers often have to suffer and to be humiliated. During this interim period the victories of God's reign cannot always be distinguished from its apparent defeats. It is only when Christ comes again that His kingdom on earth will be visibly established. His power will be beyond challenge. Then finally, all nations will acknowledge Him as their Lord and in His service find their salvation.

It is in this historical tension, marked by the clear distinction between the "already" and the "not yet," that we as His Church are called to fulfill God's mission. We proclaim that salvation which Christ by His crucifixion and death has already wrought for us. We persuade men and women to be reconciled to God in Christ. We urge His disciples to gather together in Christian churches. The Church in its mission is called by faith to establish the reality of what the earthly Jesus sought to accomplish and what the risen Christ is constantly reenacting. This was quite adequately expressed by the Second Assembly of the World Council of Churches in Evanston, 1954:

> To evangelize is to participate in His life and in His ministry to the world. This ministry is the ministry of the risen and ascended Christ: Christ as He is today. It is the ministry of God become man, by which God's Kingdom is come among men. It is the ministry of Christ's life on earth by which God is revealed as the Father. It is the ministry of His death on the Cross by which the sin of the world is taken away. It is the ministry of His resurrection by

which the powers of death and evil have been decisively defeated. It is the ministry of the heavenly Intercessor who does not will that any should perish. It is the ministry of the coming Christ by whose mercy and judgment the world is governed even now.[3]

In all its aspects, Christian service must be determined by what Christ did in the world and what He is still doing. The ministry of Christians cannot comprise anything which in its content or spirit contradicts the ministry of Christ in the "already" and the "not yet." Christ alone is the master, the content, the authority, the norm, but also the limitation of our mission. Through their ministry, Christians must change the world, insofar as Christ Himself has changed it by His work. But they also must disassociate themselves from this evil world which according to the plan of God stands under the judgment of the coming Lord and is going to pass away. Christians, therefore, must neither preach nor hope for things which are not promised to them for this interim period. Rather they must define their mission by the criteria which Christ Himself used in His ministry.

What, then, is the precise task of the mission to which we are called in Christ? Let me answer this question, and complete the chapter by proposing four theses:

A MISSION WHICH GLORIFIES GOD

Thesis 1: We are called and sent to glorify the reign of God and to manifest His saving work before the whole world.

We must put sentiment to one side. Missions' primary concern is not man, but God Himself. Today this fact is often overlooked, sometimes even denied. Mission may not become the advocate of the world, but rather must remain God's advocate in the world. In the Old Testament, the climax of the universal eschatological vision is the statement that the nations will praise God. In the New Testament, Christ summarizes His ministry on earth by saying: "I have glorified Thee on the earth" (John 17:4), and then just before His imminent death and resurrection he adds the request "now glorify Thou Me, Father, with

Thine own glory which I had in Thy presence before the world existed" (John 17:5).

In recognition of His obedience unto death by which Jesus had honored the Father and demonstrated His inviolable holiness, the Father now magnifies the Son. He exalts Him on the throne and bestows to Him all power in heaven and on earth. There He shall rule until every knee in heaven and on earth and under the earth shall bow in His name, and every tongue shall confess that Jesus Christ is Lord, to the glory of the Father (Phil. 2:10-11). The rule of Christ has not reached its goal until all enemies have become subject to Him. Therefore the whole history of mission can be summed up in the progressive fulfillment of Psalm 110:1: "The Lord has said to my Lord 'Sit at my right hand until I make Thy enemies a footstool for Thy feet'."

Thus mission includes both the service of Christ through His followers and also the service His followers render to Him as their Lord. Today it is extremely important to emphasize the priority of this doxological aim before all other aims of mission. Our one-sided concern with man and his society threatens to pervert mission and make it a secular or even a quasi-atheistic undertaking. We are living in an age of apostasy where man arrogantly makes himself the measuring rod of all things. Therefore, it is a part of our missionary task courageously to confess before all enemies of the cross that the earth belongs to God and to His anointed. This makes faithfulness in mission meaningful even where whole nations and spheres of power like the Muslim world or Maoist China have hardened themselves against the claims of the Gospel. Our task in mission is to uphold the banner of the risen Lord before the whole world, because it is His own.

A MISSION WHICH BRINGS ETERNAL REDEMPTION

Thesis 2: We are called and sent to save all men from the eternal and temporal consequences of their apostasy from God.

This thesis is a safeguard against the tendency to become inhuman in our formulation of mission theology.

One of the titles of dignity which the New Testament most frequently gives to Christ is the word *soter,* i.e. savior. Even more frequently the aim of His ministry is described by the verb "to save" or the noun "salvation."

Contemporary ecumenical mission thought has focused on the theme "Salvation Today." Ecumenical theologians frequently invoke the Old Testament word, *s h a l o m* by which they mean all that is involved in peace, harmony, and prosperity. This is designed to give more expression to the idea of fulfillment in life here and now. This is undoubtedly what people eagerly desire. It permits expression of the new horizon of hope which the Christian message has opened up for them.

But while recognizing this, we must not overlook the fact that the two New Testament terms used to describe the concept of salvation refer to another, much more important, dimension. The word *s o t e r i a* first of all is concerned with the salvation of the sinner who, because of his guilt is threatened by eternal death. The other word, *e i r e n e* (peace) describes the reconciliation with God, whose wrath may decree eternal death. Only the sacrificial death of God's Son could avert this punishment from mankind.

Traditionally the motive of saving men from eternal death has been the driving force of both Catholic and Protestant mission. The frightening vision of thousands of Chinese souls which daily, Niagara-like, plunged into an abyss so depressed Hudson Taylor that he became the motivating force behind the founding of the China Inland Mission. Today, however, a strong movement brings man's temporal well-being into the foreground. Of course, temporal "shalom" is an essential consequence of eternal salvation, but it can never produce eternal salvation. Perhaps in the ecumenical movement we are seeing in part a reaction against some spiritualistic over-emphasis of the past. But the movement is still an alarming symptom of our modern immanentism. It was the Rev. J.R.W. Stott, the main spokesman for British evangelicals, who in Uppsala reprimanded the delegates with this moving statement:

> The Assembly was preoccupied with the hunger, poverty and injustices of the contemporary world. I myself was deeply moved and challenged by it. I

do not want to see this diminished. What worried me, is that I found no comparable compassion or concern for the spiritual hunger of the unevangelized millions . . . The Lord sent His Church to preach the good news and make disciples, but I did not see the Assembly eager to obey this command of His. This same Lord wept over the unrepentant city which had rejected him; but I did not see the Assembly weeping any similar tears! [4]

It is important to underscore this timely reminder. It would be unfortunate if Christian missions would follow the widespread trend to regard reconciliation with God, which Christ wrought on our behalf, merely as a theoretical presupposition for a kind of socio-political involvement. It would be fatal to regard that involvement as the primary purpose of mission.

Perhaps it is well also to warn of the opposite extreme. There are, indeed, some missionaries concerned with little but the dread of an eternal death. Therefore they care very little about the social consequences which inevitably must emerge from forgiveness of sins. They thus jeopardize even the spiritual fruit among the receivers of their message. This much is obvious: in the New Testament reconciliation between God and man is the very heart of the vocation of Christ's ambassadors. But it is equally obvious that our being reconciled with God is authenticated by our brotherly love, without which the love of God cannot be preached.

A MISSION WHICH EXORCIZES DEMONS

Thesis 3: We are called and sent in the power of Christ's victory to disarm the evil one.

Yet another aspect of Christ's Great Commission touches on man's spiritual and social needs. When Jesus sent His twelve apostles out for the first time, "Calling His twelve disciples to Him, He gave them power over depraved spirits to cast them out. . ." (Matt. 10:1).

All four gospels tell us that a considerable part of the ministry of Jesus involved exorcizing demons. Through that He made it evident that the Kingdom of God was present in His ministry. According to I John 3:8, the

44

reason for the coming of the Son of God was to destroy the works of the devil. Thus we can conclude that the path of Christ's missionaries must also be marked by the progressive dethroning of Satanic forces. As Westerners we are often proud of our enlightenment. We have to be especially careful, therefore, not to deny the real existence of these trans-subjective personal powers. Even in our Western countries we are meeting them in the rapidly-spreading practice of occultism and spiritism.

But today we encounter demonic powers even more in rationalist and religious movements which are driven by a spirit hostile to the Spirit of Christ. They manage to make inroads into the churches, subtly dissolving their doctrinal and moral foundations, and therefore threatening them with ultimate destruction.

Every missionary knows that the conversion of the heathen is complete only when it includes the expulsion of the demons which enslaved him in his former religion. John calls Satan "the prince of this world." This means that he not only works in individuals, but that even the structures of human society are demonized, although they at the same time manifest the divine order of preservation. Anthropologists know that primal social systems cannot be changed by socio-economic reforms alone. They are reinforced by deeply-embedded sacral rights and taboos guarded over by the ancestral spirits.

Secularized ecumenical theology has coined the word "desacralization" and regards it as a fruit of the Gospel. The truth in this observation would better be expressed by the word "de-demonization." In any case we can only accept so-called secularization as a direct or indirect success in missionary work if it really involves dethroning the demons and subjecting these realms to the rule of God. If, however, secularization consists merely of a process of rationalization, this will soon lead to a new demonization, usually in the form of people being captured by ideologies. Thus, it is also part of the exorcistic aim of our mission to unmask the taboos which guard the inhuman system of racism. Here we are sent into a real battle which cannot be won by revolutionary means but only by spiritual weapons. We will return to this in the final chapter. This is what Paul has in mind when he writes to the Corinthians:

45

> For while we spend our life in a body of flesh, we
> do not war with carnal weapons. For the weapons
> of our warfare are not physical, but they are power-
> ful with God's help for the tearing down of fortresses,
> inasmuch as we tear down reasonings and every proud
> barrier that is raised up against the knowledge of God
> and lead every thought into subjection to Christ.
> (2 Cor. 10:3-5).

Here is one of the most relevant statements of the entire
New Testament dealing with the current question of how
to revolutionize inhuman social structures.

A MISSION WHICH PREPARES CHRIST'S RETURN

Thesis 4: The Church of Christ as the bridgehead of
His universal reign is called and sent to witness to the
Gospel before all mankind in preparation for the return of
our Lord.

Ever since Paul embarked on his apostolic journeys,
Christian mission has been characterized by a peculiar
restlessness. One of the distinguishing marks of all
great pioneers in mission was a holy impatience. I am
thinking of men like Raymond Lull, Francis Xavier,
Ludwig Nomminsen, Hudson Taylor, or C.T. Studd. They
never could be satisfied with what they had accomplished.
They felt compelled to move on into the still unevangelized
fields of the earth. This restlessness can be detected
as marking the beginning of every new era of mission.
Even in the smallest village congregation in Scotland or
the Black Forest of Germany the friends of missions
impatiently waited for news about other historic openings
for the proclamation of the Gospel to non-Christian peoples.
Such restlessness can partially be explained by anxiety
for the eternal state of the lost. But it is characteristic
as well of missionaries like Count von Zinzendorf who,
during the present eon, did not expect any great number of
conversions, but only the gathering of the first-fruits among
all peoples.

An alarming sign of our times is that we do not sense
much of that holy restlessness in our churches. True,
people become restless when they look into the near
future. Many are even discussing the phenomenon of future

shock. But the cause of such restlessness is the prediction of such things as population explosions, world-wide famines, or the outbreak of an atomic war. There is cause for real concern, to be sure. But the greater danger is to become so engaged with this-worldly problems that we lose the vision of the real goal of history. This divine goal of our present age is the return of Christ and the establishment of His Kingdom over all nations of our earth. However, even this is not the absolute and final goal of the plan of the triune God. For He aims at nothing less than creating a totally new heaven and a totally new earth (Rev. 21:1).

Prior to this God must be manifested on this old earth before the eyes of all men as leading it to its destination in Christ. He is going to prove that in virtue of the victory which Christ gained over sin, death, and the devil, even visible dominion over all the powers and nations of our earth has been given to Him. This great and joyful fact should inspire Christians in everything they hope, talk, and do. It should encourage us to serve Christ in a world full of creative ideas. It must be manifested both in our visible existence as the community of the redeemed, and in our ministry of reconciliation within society. We should thereby inform the world that its hopes for the future will find both their fulfillment and their judgment in the rule of Christ, already established among the believers. We all are called to burn ourselves out in the ministry of reconciliation in the name of Jesus Christ. Every Christian must participate in the missionary witness of the coming kingdom. Forms and functions are not of primary importance. But is is indispensable that motives and aims remain clear, and that we are always ready to respond as God moves.

We confess that daily we experience failures in our efforts to make peace. This makes us aware that during this present age the kingdom of universal peace and social justice can be realized only to a limited extent. The most we can expect are signs, transitory results. Our best efforts are daily counteracted by the prince of this world. Through the person of the Antichrist he will still achieve an almost total triumph over the whole of mankind toward the close of this age. The messianic reign on earth will be established only when Jesus returns

47

to be united with His Church. It is to this glorious day that the eyes of all those inspired by the prophecies of the Bible are directed.

That day, however, cannot come before all peoples of earth have had the Gospel preached to them. Therefore world mission remains the chief function of the Church. The decisive question directed to us is, whether we are ready to heed the call for missionary involvement. There are many signs which indicate that this call now reaches us for perhaps the last time before the doors to the world of nations are definitely closed.

"Happy is that servant whom his master finds doing so when he arrives" (Matt. 24:46).

4

The Crucial Issue of Mission and Humanization

World mission, world history and social change are inseparably interrelated in a dialectical tension. Both the motive and the goal of world mission is the Kingdom of God. In spite of growing resistance, this Kingdom is also the goal of world history, and even now it is seeking to permeate human society. The Kingdom in power and glory, has always been the conscious objective of Christian missions. And missions are always reminded that their obedience to the Great Commission is tested by their responsiveness to the opportunities of world history. For if God is the ruler of both world history and mission history, it follows that He directs world history in such a way that the world is continually confronted in fluctuating situations with the offer of salvation in Christ. Thus the Church in mission has the task in each historic moment of discovering the opportunities God provides to testify to the non-Christian world about His whole purpose of love. Thus she will firmly keep in mind that this purpose looks beyond the preservation of the world to its final salvation.

Two major conflicting approaches to this task, each represented by a respectable missionary force, have been developed recently. Unfortunately they seem to be unable to find each other in a constructive synthesis.

One of them is the evangelical approach. Consistent with the tradition of Protestant world missions as a whole, evangelicals (I am speaking of those with a statesman-like vision) would look for new opportunities where God has prepared populations responsive to the Gospel. Here evangelicals would mobilize as strong a missionary force as possible both from the indigenous churches nearby and also through missionaries from the larger churches in the West in order to secure a maximum of new disciples. Evangelicals used to call such openings "revivals" and ascribed them solely to the work of the Holy Spirit.

Today, while not diminishing the stress on prevenient grace which is at work in such group movements, many evangelicals would admit that sociological factors also may play an important part. This is, at least, the conviction underlying the world-wide research centered at the Institute of Church Growth at Fuller Theological Seminary in Pasadena, California. Anthropological and historical questions are treated with no less scholarship than theology and biblical missionary methods. There they seek to discover where present conditions make non-Christian peoples responsive to the gospel message. These situations would be the main concentration points of a wise strategy of mission. [1]

Such a concept was officially adopted by missions belonging to the Interdenominational Foreign Mission Association and the Evangelical Foreign Missions Association at the Wheaton Congress on the World-Wide Mission of the Church in 1966. Regretting their former "complacency with small results long after a larger response could have been the norm" and their "failure to take full advantage of the response of receptive peoples," the Wheaton Declaration urged "that research be carried out by nationals and missionaries in all parts of the world to learn why churches are or are not growing. . . to evaluate church growth opportunities now overlooked, and to review the role, methods, and expenditures of our agencies in the light of their significance to evangelism and church growth." [2]

This strategy combines the theologically valid conviction of the absolute priority of eternal salvation with a new understanding of history as a dynamic process which conditions the *kairoi toon ethnoon,* i.e., the opportunities arising when whole peoples become responsive to the proclamation of the Gospel.

This evangelical view not only shares the soteriological concern of the early apostles but it is also verified today by major ethnic movements which can and do contribute greatly to the multiplication of church membership in many parts of the world. Contrary to the popular impression that the advance of the world missionary movement has been brought to a standstill by nationalism and renascent indigenous religions, evangelicals point out from a growing data base that the Church today faces missionary opportunities as seldom before in its entire history.

In Africa during the years 1950-1970 the number of Christians has risen from 20 to 50 million. In Indonesia from 1966 to 1968 alone 400,000 people applied for church membership, and the movement is still going on. One might object that the Indonesian phenomenon has more political than spiritual causes. But this is exactly our point: in mission history we find it impossible to divide the motives and factors which condition the process of Christianization. The decisive question for the Church is whether she is willing to respond to the opportunities which God as the ruler of history presents to her. The Gospel has the inherent power to transform even an inquirer who first requests baptism with very mixed and doubtful motives. If this were not true, Europe would always have remained a heathen continent!

Evangelical leaders are concerned that within many churches and mission societies the awareness of such evangelistic opportunities is on the decline. As a matter of fact — as far as Western churches are concerned — the old evangelistic incentive to preach the Gospel to those who have never heard it, "for the opening of their eyes and their turning from darkness to light and from the authority of Satan to God, to obtain forgiveness of sins and their allotted portion among those made holy through faith in Me" (Acts 26:18), now seems to be a decisive motivation for missionary service only in evangelical mission societies. Organizations such as the World-Wide Evangelization Crusade and the United Mission to Nepal are still moved by the concern for unevangelized areas in the world which have been newly opened up for mission work.

THE HUMANISTIC APPROACH

Within the other churches, and not the least within those missions which are affiliated with the Comission of World Mission and Evangelism of the World Council of Churches, the evangelistic drive seems to have been more or less displaced by socio-ethical concern. At least since the preparation for the Uppsala Assembly of 1968, not Christianization and church planting, but humanization and radical change of social structures seem to be the new ecumenical missionary strategy. In the *Drafts for Sections* "Renewal and Mission" the place formerly given to the mission fields was dedicated to the "points of tension within contemporary human existence,"[3] which means to racial strife, social upheaval or student revolts in all parts of the world. Achieving more satisfactory horizontal relations seems to have gained the upper hand over against Paul's interpretation of his apostolic ministry: "We beg you for Christ's sake, to be reconciled to God." (2 Cor. 5:20). Concern caused by such apparent "displacement of their primary tasks" in ecumenical missions, as the Frankfurt Declaration later called it, caused McGavran to put the searching question to all Assembly delegates: "Will Uppsala betray the two billion?"[4]

In terms of this provocative question, converting non-Christians or rendering social service emerged as a polarization. The false impression arose that the alternatives were in fact mutually exclusive. One or the other was vigorously attacked by some and defended by others, leading to the strong divisions between "evangelicals" and "ecumenicals," "traditionalists" and "progressives" which marked the heated deliberations in Section II.

Note that the two tasks of proclamation and service are not mutually exclusive in view of the total commission of the Church. They need not be considered as alternatives in the task of mission. J. R. W. Stott, in an issue of *Church Growth Bulletin* published after Uppsala, proposed this formula: "Evangelicals should proclaim the equation that 'mission equals witness plus service'." [5]

As a matter of fact there is a legitimate way today to view missions in their socio-historical context. Newly-opened geographical and ethnic areas provide missions a vital opportunity to meet the challenge of history. There are wholly untouched tribes in the valleys of Central New Guinea, on the heights of the Himalayas, in the primeval forests of the Amazon, and in other places where the touch of cultural contact calls for a new pioneering missionary enterprise.

NEW FORMS OF MISSION

But we must also consider situations which are not "pioneer mission," but which demand new forms of mission to open new areas by witness and service. I would mention only three examples to illustrate the point:

1. One of the catch-words in Asia and Africa today is the term "nation building." Similar problems in India are called "communalism," in Africa "tribalism." As N. Sithole[6] has shown, missions themselves helped create the spiritual foundations of modern nationalism in Africa. But since nationalism in its initial stage has been a reactionary movement against Western colonialism, much of its unifying force has now been dissipated in the newly independent states. Thus, from the past, the old unresolved frictions of tribes and castes are again emerging. They frustrate the unifying efforts of national governments and can cause horrible fratricidal wars, such as we have recently seen in Nigeria. Who is able to invoke a spiritual force powerful enough to reconcile such dissensions? Here national and regional Christian Councils have had a word to say which has been taken seriously by many national governments.

2. Young nations are forced to introduce *industrialization* in order to solve their economic problems. But industrialization produces estrangement from the familiar patterns of life and brings forth new social antagonism. Who will help the factory laborer find meaning in his job at the conveyor belt? Who will encourage the disparate groups to see each other not as opponents but as partners? Who will exhort management not to sacrifice human per-

sonality on the altar of productivity and efficiency? All these questions point to the growing significance of industrial mission in many parts of the world.

3. Industrialization inevitably produces *urbanization* in our age of automatic production, the migratory labor force often exceeds the market for new jobs. In the slums of Calcutta, Bangkok, Lagos, and Rio de Janeiro the cities are surrounded by septic belts of an uprooted proletariat with all predictable hygienic, social and moral evils. Who helps to alleviate these emergency situations and to integrate these stranded persons into the new society as respected citizens? The answer of the National Christian Council of Kenya, for example, was the creation of a number of exemplary community centers in Nairobi, built in partnership with the cooperating missions.

These three examples may serve to show how the social and political problems of nations today raise genuine questions as to whether Christian missions might be able to mobilize sufficient spiritual forces to meet them. Giving aid to people in emergency or in a developmental crisis out of the love of Christ, overcoming old or new enmities through the power of reconciliation, witnessing courageously on behalf of the dignity of all discriminated persons because Jesus died for them — all these are opportunities where the verbal proclamation of the gospel can be authenticated by the serving fellowship of love, thus demonstrating its winning power.

I myself once saw in a Nairobi Community Center how Christian help towards the social integration of stranded tribal migrants made them very receptive to the Christian message. Each Sunday three services in different vernaculars had to be held at this center. They were so crowded that loudspeakers had to be used for the people who could not find room in the church.

In the countries of the Third World the Christian mission still meets many people who are fully prepared to listen to a religious interpretation of their social need at its deepest level. These people are aware that a new culture needs an integrating religious center. The social challenges are at the same time opportunities for genuine evangelism.

Thus we find that the two ways of approaching missionary

strategy need not be mutually exclusive. If mission means crossing new frontiers, there is no reason why these frontiers should be defined only in geographical and ethnic ways. To cross social and historic frontiers can be a very legitimate missionary challenge as well.

ECUMENICAL THEOLOGICAL DEVIATIONS

What is the decisive reason for the apparent polarization of the two concepts of missionary strategy? Why have they not been able to meet each other in a complimentary synthesis?

I do not think that the main reason lies in the area of policy. It is rather the conviction on the part of evangelicals that present ecumenical attempts to redefine the goal of mission in terms of humanizing the social structure reveal a decisive theological deviation which strikes at the very heart of the Christian faith. The shock of the deliberations in Uppsala Section II, where evangelicals had to struggle with all their might to introduce such elementary Christian convictions as the need for a new birth, will not easily be forgotten. It took Canon Douglas Webster three strenuous attempts to introduce a reference to the two billion who had never fully heard the Christian message, and even then it was reluctantly accepted in a diluted form.[7] According to Webster, the weakness of the report "is less in what it said, than in what it refused to say."[8]

Why was there such a resistance to including statements which only sought to affirm the central concern of Christian missions accepted since the days of the apostles? Could it be that social consciousness has swallowed up soteriological compassion? Could it be that the dogmatic convictions underlying such soteriological compassion have faded away, at least with some of the most vociferous protagonists of humanization?

We must realize that openness to the historical situation runs the risk that Christian mission might be led astray. In world history we do not encounter the *Deus revelatus* but the *Deus absconditus*. And far too easily we forget that in world history the rule of Christ is still contested by the prince of this world.

In past ages missions were susceptible to a possible confusion of evangelism and imperialism. Our temptation today is that Christians yield to the voice of syncretistic tolerance and go about their "mission" silently "with no ulterior motives," as it is said. But by so doing they unwittingly subject themselves to still other motives which their non-Christian acquaintances most tenaciously keep in mind.

The malady which many of our major missions have never dared to examine closely is the insidious paralysis of biblical convictions of prominent churchmen. Critical methods of exegetical research have undermined the authority of Scripture. Demythologization and existential interpretation have dissolved the concept of Christ's expiatory sacrifice and the reality of His future kingdom still to be established in power by His second coming. Situationalist views of biblical ethics reduce its texts to the level of answers to antiquated socio-political problems. What remain are some vague principles, like responsibility, solidarity, and openness for the future, completely abstracted from the specific history of revelation and salvation in which they occur.

Even Jesus becomes only the prototype of an ideal social attitude, the "man for others." His resurrection and lordship means scarcely more than that the community of His followers may still be inspired by His example. Christological affirmations are thus abstracted from the living person of Christ and interpreted as reflections of the Church about her own mission. The conclusion drawn by some members of a missiological seminar under the guidance of a well-known ecumenical theologian sounds like this:

> The traditional statements about the Return of Christ, that God be all in all, and the like, aim functionally at man's becoming man, a goal to which Christ is calling and paving the way, but which it is not given for man to reach on his own. [9]

By such theological methods biblical prophecies are deprived of their realistic content. While their form and their original content may not be directly negated, a process of philosophical or sociological abstraction transforms them into anthropocentric statements which in spirit and wording appear merely to be reflections of a current humanistic ideology.

This general theological situation views the primacy of verbal witness in Christian mission with increasing scepticism.

MISSION WITHOUT PROCLAMATION

We now encounter the strange concept that the socially desirable consequences of the Gospel would still allow us to call our task "mission" even if we deliberately abstain from calling upon people to believe in Christ and to be baptized in His name. To quote the findings of the above-mentioned study group once again:

> . . . it cannot be regarded as the goal of Christian mission to 'make' non-Christians Christian, to 'convert' them, or to 'win' them. To practice the function of the Christian faith—in a theoretically responsible way—is the only method of spreading it. . . to communicate Christian ideas (e.g. of 'God,' 'sin') and practices (e.g. prayer, worship, baptism, eucharist), without being asked, to non-Christians and children, is an obstacle to mission. (The Christian education of children is always authoritarian. To abandon it would be a sign of shalom.) [10]

The argument for "mission without proclamation" is that any form of humanization stresses the authority of Christ. Even if this is not done expressly, a humanizing process such as breaking down the barriers of caste in Indian school classes can only go on by the power of the risen Christ, who is understood to be the anonymously directing power of world history. Thus it does not matter which group actually brings about the desirable social change, be they Christians, Marxists, Humanists, or Neo-Hindus. World history is understood as the result of God's mission, and in the transformation of the social structures we are said to realize the features of the coming Kingdom of God. The conclusion follows easily: any actual engagement as such is already mission, meaning the participation in the *Missio Dei* in world history.

What we observe here is a most dangerous shortcut in theological reasoning. Theology of mission is no longer clearly focused on two indispensable biblical data: the crucifixion and the second coming of Christ. The dialectical tension between world history and salvation history, expressed by these two events, is overlooked. Church and mission are reduced to the dimension of the world. In such a concept the eschatological Kingdom of Christ is swallowed up by the immanent achievements of historical evolution. Even if such evolution is ascribed to the work of the anonymous Christ, we are nearer to the monistic philosophy of history of Hegel and Karl Marx than to the prophecies of the Bible.

SOCIETY OR SALVATION

Does such a theological position really sacrifice something indispensable? Is it not true that the coming Kingdom is manifested when social structures are humanized according to the will of God? Should we not be glad to observe that a number of contemporary political ideologies and syncretistic movements have received their dynamic direction by being influenced by the prophetic faith of Christianity? Should we not even admit that some secular liberation movements seem to be more genuine fruits of Christian mission than many sterile younger churches? Should we not even support the revolutionary movements as our missionary partners in the struggle for justice in the world?

Acute observers like Walter Freytag and Lesslie Newbigin stated long ago that most revolutionary movements bear messianic features. Some of them have even produced their own political and/or religious messiahs. They have been described in terms borrowed from Jesus of Nazareth in His struggle, suffering, death, and resurrection. Here Christian missions seemingly have achieved an exciting effect which they would never have anticipated!

What hinders us from recognizing such unexpected results as legitimate fruits of mission? Why can we not really rejoice at this transformation of history which may exceed by far the social results of missions? The reason is that the ultimate aim of these movements is a perfect society in which there is neither demand nor room for salvation. Humanization has superseded evangelization. Man places himself in the center. He declares himself to be the measuring rod of all things and creates for himself a paradise without God. He is not in need of any God since he is replacing God. This "theology of the serpent" is, according to Ernst Bloch,[11] the secret atheistic theme of the Bible. "Ye shall be like God" pits the emancipation of man against the concept of a sovereign God. Here Bloch echoes Karl Marx who, in 1841, wrote in the introduction to his doctoral thesis:

> The confession of Prometheus: "With one single word, I hate all gods" is the confession of philosophy itself, its verdict against all celestial or terrestrial gods, who do not acknowledge the human self-consciousness as the highest deity. There shall be nobody besides him. [12]

Being aware of this inherent atheistic thread running through the history of humanism, we are shocked to see how naively current ecumenical missiology can take up the concept of humanization and put it one-sidedly into the center of its motivation and goal. True enough, the New Testament does describe Jesus as the New Man and the beginner of a new humanity. But this is only complementary to the more basic concept that in Jesus Christ we meet the pre-existent Son of God, who wrought our salvation and who is risen to receive our worship and obedience. Separating these two concepts and allowing His human nature to dominate the foreground always runs the risk of perverting the Christian faith into a humanistic syncretism. It tends to remove the ontological diastasis between biblical faith and non-Christian religions and ideologies. We are exhorted along with the adherents of other "living faiths" to discover the manhood of man.

MISSIOLOGICAL BANKRUPTCY

There is one notable text in recent ecumenical documents which goes to an extreme in separating the concept of humanization from the doxological and soteriological context of biblical faith. It occurred first in the American contribution to *The Church for Others* and was quoted in the commentary to the *Draft for Section II* in Uppsala 1968.

59

We have lifted up humanization as the goal of mission because we believe that more than others it communicates in our period of history the meaning of the messianic goal. In another time the goal of God's redemptive work might best have been described in terms of man turning towards God rather than in terms of God turning towards man. . . The fundamental question was that of the true God, and the Church responded to that question by pointing to him. It was assuming that the purpose of mission was Christianization, bringing man to God through Christ and his church. Today the fundamental question is much more that of true man, and the dominant concern of the missionary congregation must therefore be to point to the humanity of Christ as the goal of mission.[13]

Here, it seems to me, we encounter nothing less than the bankruptcy of responsible missionary theology. No longer does being a missionary mean to be the herald of a sovereign Lord who has entrusted to him an unchangeable message. The eternal life or death of the hearers no longer hangs in the balance. Instead the concerns of the hearers themselves determine the scope and content of the message. In former ages people were more religious, they asked for the true God, and so Christian missions directed them to Him. Today, however, people do not care for gods any more, but for better human relations. Thus mission no longer speaks of God but directs them to the humanity of Christ as the goal of history!

All this is done in the concern of missionary accommodation. By confining ourselves to the concept of humanization we hope to find a field of common concern with Hindus, Muslims, Marxists, and Humanists. For, according to the concept of the anonymous Christ *extra muros ecclesiae,* we are already sharing in Christ if we together with them work for the humanization of mankind. Perhaps, by means of dialogue, if the others perchance ask us for the motive of our actions, they might even become disposed to accept Christ and to integrate Him into their present faiths.

But when arguing like this one overlooks the fact that missionary proclamation calls for a wholehearted decision. It is not possible to say "yes" to the gift and

60

remain indifferent to the Giver. It is possible, however, to reach out for the gift and to say "no" to the Giver. This is what all post-Christian religions and ideologies have done. They have borrowed principles and visions from the Christian message to enrich or transform their own previous systems. Thus, when engaging in dialogue with representatives of such syncretistic movements, we will always discover a certain area of contact with them as far as situational analyses, general principles, and visions of hope are concerned. But all these conversations, including the Christian-Marxist dialogue, come to a sudden end when we speak of Christ and Him crucified. Ernst Bloch may place His cross within the row of the thousand crosses of Spartacus at the Via Appia. But this is far from accepting the cross as the altar at which our guilt was expiated and our peace with God was restored. There is no bridge which spans the gap between a social concept of humanization and the biblical mystery that by Christ's sacrifice not only were we restored to our true humanity, but we also were made children of God and partakers of His divine life.

Because of this rejection of the unique claim of Christ, all post-Christian movements betray to one degree or another an anti-Christian character. Thus their ultimate destination is to prepare for the final dramatic conflict with the community of Christ, where the dominating figure will be the Antichrist. He will personify a Christless humanization program by appearing to be Christ himself. He will unite the whole of humanity under his rule, a rule which will superficially appear to be a paradise of social justice. But this paradise will end up in terror, blood, and tears.

One basic error in a theology of mission which locates the missionary work of God one-dimensionally in world history is to belittle the demonological crack which runs right through history from the fall to the end of the world. It is therefore unable to put the cross of Christ in the center. The propitiatory purpose of the cross is overlooked. This also waters down its present ethical significance: that we must endure our own cross and the growing antagonism of the world in view of Christ's final triumph in history at His second coming.

There is no direct road leading from present world injustices through the transformation of all social structures to some utopic humanity, equated with the messianic goal. The Bible clearly teaches us that world history finds its way toward salvation only through obedience and faith in Christ. Where, however, the world rejects His offer of grace and His royal authority, it definitely falls under the wrath of God and proceeds toward its final judgment. Mission, according to Lesslie Newbigin, is the cutting edge which God introduces into the stream of history.[14] By this edge people are forced to make their decision about Christ. Thus the saved new humanity and the doomed old age are separated. The specific mandate of mission is to erect the cross of Christ in ever new human spheres of life. This cross is the power of salvation for those who believe, but an odor of death among those who are perishing (2 Cor. 2:15, 16).

Fully aware of these two exit-routes at the end of world history, Christian mission will still rejoice at all truly humanizing changes in society. We evaluate them as direct or indirect effects of the ministry of reconciliation and as anticipatory reflections of the coming Kingdom.

But abiding salvation is to be found only where people who were alienated from God are rescued and incorporated into the body of Christ. This determines the priorities of our missionary functions and keeps alive our hope in the coming Christ. Only Christ Himself will resolve the dialectical tension between world history and mission history. He will remove their tragic dichotomy by His final victory over the anti-Christian cataclysm of world history. Then the common goal of world history and mission history, the Kingdom in power and glory will definitely be established.

5

The Story of the Frankfurt Declaration

In preceding chapters, the adoption of the Frankfurt Declaration on March 4, 1970, was mentioned. Only a few people ever realized that its full title is the "Frankfurt Declaration on the Fundamental Crisis in Christian Mission." But most people who have heard of it have become quite aware that it deals with this crisis. For the preceding 10 or 15 years many books and articles had been written, and many lectures had been delivered about the crisis in missions. But none of these stirred up a commotion comparable to the almost explosive reaction to the Frankfurt Declaration. When it appeared, curiously, some of the very people who had been writing and lecturing on their own interpretation of the crisis reacted by beginning to raise doubts as to whether such a crisis in mission existed after all. What was the reason for this unexpected change of mind?

In contrast to the previous descriptions of the postwar crisis in missions, the Frankfurt Declaration attempted a much more radical diagnosis. It did not describe the root of this crisis as located primarily in changing historical conditions or in the captivity of missions within outdated structures. Rather it claimed that the real damage was caused by a crack in the foundation of mission itself, namely an insidious falsification of the basic assumptions of the Christian faith. This diagnosis could not be bypassed easily. It could be substantiated by others with similar apprehensions. It could shock some by making them aware of the seriousness of the situation. Or still others could take it to be an attack on some fashionable theories of mission. It was a document that could not be ignored. Consequently the Frankfurt Declaration soon received a measure of attention which the first signers had not anticipated.

HOW IT STARTED

I vividly remember my deep shock when in February, 1968, I first read the *Draft for Section II* of the World Council of Churches Assembly to be held in Uppsala in July of that year. The title of that draft, designed by the staff of the Department of World Mission and Evangelism in Geneva, was "Renewal in Mission." But it immediately appeared to me to represent not a renewal, but a total distortion of mission. It represented a serious disruption of the whole tradition of missiological thinking embodied in the documents of the preceding world missionary conferences from Edinburgh 1910 to Mexico City in 1963.

Since that shock I have now learned to look more critically at the ambiguity of those earlier statements. But up to then I had been a sincere adherent of the ecumenical cause which had attracted so many of the great charismatic church leaders of this century. The next morning I said to my students, "This Geneva draft will either be outrightly rejected by the Assembly delegates in Uppsala, or it will be changed beyond recognition."

Although I am no prophet, I felt very close to being one at that time. I soon discovered that I was not the only one annoyed by this unusual statement produced by Walter Hollenweger and his associates. Protests came from many sides. A group of Scandinavian mission leaders composed an alternative draft. Many proposals for major amendment came in from other countries. Just in time for the meeting of the Fourth Assembly of the World Council of Churches Donald McGavran published his thought-provoking article "Will Uppsala Betray the Two Billion?"

This article revealed that he and I were kindred spirits and in our subsequent correspondence the idea arose that German missionary leaders should do something similar to what American evangelical missions had done two years previously when they drew up their famous Wheaton Declaration.

Why was there still need for a second document of this kind? In fact it has rightly been observed that the Wheaton Declaration anticipated most points of the Frankfurt Declaration. In some matters the Wheaton Declaration does give more specific guidance. As to content and character, the main difference is that the Wheaton Declaration speaks to current theological and missiological issues in general, while the Frankfurt Declaration focuses attention more directly on the development of mission theology expounded in the more recent and avant-garde publications of the World Council's Commission on World Mission and Evangelism.

Another, even more important, difference is that the Wheaton Declaration is the voice of that great company of conservative evangelical missions which have already organized themselves outside of the more traditional Geneva-linked missions. The Frankfurt Declaration, on the other hand, attempts to develop its position from within the ecumenical movement and therefore seeks to readjust the entire course of that movement from the inside. As McGavran mentioned in his correspondence, this would not be the first time that German mission leaders had voiced theological objections to the pronouncements of great international missionary conferences. Under the leadership of men like Karl Heim, Karl Hartenstein and Walter Freytag, German delegations had voiced their protest both at the Jerusalem and Madras conferences of the International Missionary Council in 1928 and 1938. Finally, after World War II, they started to receive new attention for their eschatological criticism of the optimistic this-worldly conception of some theologians of mission.

Unfortunately the voice of Martin Luther's Germany was not to ring out in Uppsala's Section II. A church delegate from Sumatra, desperately advocating a mission understanding relevant to the wide-open evangelistic opportunities in Indonesia, looked in vain for support from his German colleagues. This time it was British evangelical John Stott who made the most piercing pronouncement in the Assembly, in fact succeeding to a degree to modify Uppsala's final report.

But in spite of the fact that the final pronouncement on mission adopted by the World Council made some changes in the original draft, it was far from satisfactory to the evangelical mind. The pronouncement emerged a rather clumsy and inconsistent compromise, attempting to harmonize the opinions presented in the section. It came out with a definitely secularist undertone given to it by the editorial committee.

MISSIONS : WHICH WAY ?

I did not get to Uppsala myself, although my missiological doctorate was taken there. But when I read the papers from the Assembly and received personal reports from some of the delegates, I realized that something rather dramatic needed to be done. The Commission on World Mission and Evangelism was being totally captured by the secular theology which had been a growing influence since New Delhi, 1961.

In partial response to this, I wrote a little book called, in English, *Missions: Which Way?* Two outstanding German professors of mission commended the book and it was taken by one of them as "sounding an alarm." It was designed to awaken the whole of the fellowship of German Protestant missionary societies, and to stir them into action. As member organizations of the CWME, I felt they should exercise their responsibility to correct its theological course. In the final chapter, I mentioned the necessity of the formation of a German counterpart to the Wheaton Declaration, stating:

> On the basis of this declaration, the Commission should be induced to listen to the objections and answer them in a responsible way. If the document is well-supported by many signers from all churches and missions, it could lead to a decisive theological re-orientation and a correspondingly new arrangement in the working program for the Geneva Division and its regional councils.[1]

I was grateful to find that the cry of alarm was heard. I had sent copies with personal dedications to the leader of the German Missionary Council and also to Walter Hollenweger in Geneva. At least Geneva was alarmed. A top-level delegation was sent to the German mission headquarters in Hamburg for a conference as to what should be the reaction to my book. I was not invited. The outcome was the decision to pay no public attention to the book, hoping that as a result it would pass virtually unnoticed.

Consequently, the German Missionary Council did not respond. The newly established "Conference of Evangelical Missions" would have been basically in agreement with my point of view, but at that point they were still struggling to get organized and were not prepared to enter the debate.

At this juncture, one last avenue had opened. The "Theological Convention" was a group of conservative theologians, some in academic, some in pastoral positions pulled together by the militant "No Other Gospel Movement" to provide theological leadership in our current anti-modernist struggle in Germany. At the first meeting in March, 1969, the Theological Convention had become aware that this church struggle was not merely a domestic German affair, but had already affected the whole ecumenical movement. A subcommittee on mission and ecumenics was named to keep an eye on current developments. This committee was asked to prepare a document which would clearly point out the theological issues at stake in contemporary missions. Unfortunately the committee as such never managed to meet. My draft of the proposed declaration consequently had to be circulated by correspondence. It was then discussed in the plenary meeting of the Theological Convention at Frankfurt in 1970 and, after some amendments, adopted.

A few days later the document was sent out to all German missionary societies. We asked them to test our theses on the basis of their biblical foundations and to check the accuracy of our descriptions of the current theological errors in churches, missions, and the ecumenical movement. If they agreed with what was written, we requested them to sign the declaration.

Two months later, the Frankfurt Declaration was translated into English in the Disciples' Institute in Tubingen and sent to Donald McGavran in view of a possible circulation in America. It did, indeed, appear both in the *Church Growth Bulletin* (July, 1970) and in *Christianity Today* (June 19, 1970). Because of the enthusiastic recommendations given to it by McGavran and Harold Lindsell, editor of *Christianity Today,* it soon received attention on other continents as well.

THE AIM OF THE FRANKFURT DECLARATION

The Frankfurt Declaration makes no attempt to proclaim a new theological understanding of mission by using modern philosophical categories. Nor does it grapple with current attempts to develop indigenous theologies in Asia and Africa. The practical aspects of mission strategy are not touched. It has no other aim but to reaffirm the biblical basis, content, and goal of mission which, in spite of occasional distortions, have provided the deepest motivation for the whole Protestant missionary movement from the pietistic revival until the pronouncements on mission by the Second WCC Assembly at Evanston in 1964 and the Wheaton Declaration of 1968.

The declaration is rooted in the Lutheran concept of the distinction between the objective atonement on Calvary and its subjective application by the administration of the means of grace which must be accepted by faith. This concept is to be seen in the context of the understanding of the history of redemption theology as it was developed by evangelical biblical scholars from Zinzendorf to Oscar Cullman. The authority and unity of the Scriptures are firmly upheld in the Declaration, and it attempts to avoid the destructive tendencies of higher criticism and demythologization. It is based upon the finality of God's revelation, upon His atoning work in Jesus Christ, and upon the validity of the Great Commission as the unchanging norm for our Christian outreach. Its authors are convinced that, from the time that Christ first sent out the apostles to His second coming, the missionary mandate to the Church and also the content of its message remain the same.

The Frankfurt Declaration does not attempt to develop a complete system of mission theology. Rather it articulates the biblical understanding of mission with parti-

68

cular reference to those aspects questioned today by
heretical undercurrents in church, theological, missionary,
ecumenical, and para-ecclesiastical movements. True, the
immediate objects of its criticism are the recent documents
of the CWME/WCC, especially those of the study project
on the Missionary Structures of the Church. But the
opinions voiced there are not merely the personal idiosyn-
crasies of their authors. Rather they form part of an
almost universal wave of heresy which in its threat to
the Christian Church is as dangerous as the gnostic
movement of the second century or the age of rationalism.

The most notorious elements of this theological complex include the diminishing of transcendental consciousness, the neo-rationalistic dissolution of scriptural authority, the secularist transformation of biblical statements of
faith into a sociological understanding of world and history,
the watering down of the uniqueness of biblical revelation
by pan-religious or situationalist perspectives, the syncretistic transformation of Christology and pneumatology into
general forces seen at work in the process of historical
change, the reduction of the divine nature of the Church
to a mere instrumentality, the redefinition of eschatological
prophecies as evolutionist utopias, and above all the
perilous exchange of the basic theocentric dimension of
biblical faith into a self-centered humanism.

The Frankfurt Declaration is an all-out attack on the
ecumenical program of humanization. But it does not
attack its valid point of concern for a more human, harmonious relationship between man and man in society.
Its disagreement arises at the point of the discovery that in
the final analysis the kind of humanization advocated is
not true humanization of society, but rather the humanization of God or conversely, the deification of man. The
basic Christological creed, "God became man," gives way
to the concept, already insinuated by the serpent in the
Garden of Eden, that "man becomes God."

In the theology of secularization which has become the
dominant school of thought in the ecumenical movement,
we find that the horizontal dimension of the Christian faith
almost completely overshadows the vertical. Current statements of this theology, even in spite of their use of traditional theological vocabulary, are talking about man, and

only about man and his possibilities. This theology seeks God everywhere: in the existential questions of modern man, in social change, in non-violent as well as in bloody revolutions. But it does not seek Him where He wants to be found: first, in His word which becomes flesh in Jesus Christ, and secondly in His congregation of saints, gathered around the biblical preaching and the Lord's table. Even statements referring to the death, resurrection and second coming of Jesus Christ are not primarily concerned with Christ. They use these emotion-laden words and phrases as symbols to describe the way in which the Church should become involved in society.

The authors of the Frankfurt Declaration are convinced that the issues at stake are of utmost importance to the future of the Church. The life and death of the missionary enterprise hang in the balance. The Declaration was framed to stem the tide and stop the infiltration of harmful currents into the theology of mission.

ECHOES AND SIGNATURES

When the first mimeographed copies of the Frankfurt Declaration were sent out to the German-speaking world, the tumult it immediately produced was unexpected. Small and large quantities were ordered by mission societies, church boards and synods, Christian organizations, parishes, and individuals. It appeared in several German periodicals. Soon signatures started pouring in.

Although many did sign it, many more would have if the German Missionary Council had not immediately registered its dissent. Many potential signers, in sympathy with the document, were thereby scared away.

The loudest approval came from the evangelical mission societies, both Lutheran and others. Some of the non-Lutherans felt some hesitation because they sensed a certain sacramental emphasis in the Declaration which they were not able to endorse, although they were in fundamental agreement with its missiological content.

A number of letters of appreciation revealed what people found most helpful in the Frankfurt Declaration. They indicated that it had unmasked and articulated some tendencies in contemporary theological thinking which had disquieted them previously, but which they had not been able clearly to identify. This unmasking was not confined to the realm of mission, but showed that the same humanistic and sociological ideologies had made similar inroads into all other spheres of church life.

The year following the publication of the Frankfurt Declaration was filled with many public debates in assemblies, executive committees, study groups, theological seminaries, and church synods. This effect was particularly satisfactory because for the first time in many a year the theological foundation of mission had become a major issue. For several years the changing of social structures had seemed to be the all-important subject for churches and missions. The widest result, however, was the fact that the echo of the Frankfurt Declaration came bounding back from many other countries and continents of the world. Soon the document had been translated into most other European languages. The Italian version was prepared by none other than the Vatican's *Congregatio de Propaganda Fide!* Correspondence from the U.S.A. brought almost as many signatures as we had received from Germany. Besides many evangelical mission societies, the entire Association of Evangelical Professors of Mission endorsed the Declaration. Commentaries appeared in several mission periodicals.

When, on request of the International Fellowship of Evangelical Students, I visited Japanese theological seminaries in 1971, doors to churches and missions in several other countries of Asia and Australia opened for my ministry. In most places the first topic requested was an introduction to the Frankfurt Declaration. Meanwhile it had also been translated into Asian languages such as Japanese, Chinese, Indonesian, and Pakistani. I found that the Frankfurt Declaration produced the same polarizing effect in Asia as it had in Germany. Some deplored it as regrettable divisionism, others welcomed it as a necessary instrument to discern the spirits. Personally I rejoiced that largely on the basis of the Frankfurt Declaration, a worldwide brotherhood was emerging, of people who had found themselves to be involved in similar theological and ecclesiastical struggles. They now realized that they had been correct in their apprehensions and critical diagnoses of the present ecumenical trend which (though it had appeared to some to be overwhelming) was in reality weak and basically erroneous.

THE GENEVA COLD SHOULDER

From only one major quarter no public reaction was heard. This was the very body to which the Frankfurt Declaration had been directed, the World Council of Churches and its mission department (CWME). In an interview with a German Christian journalist, Philip Potter, Director of CWME, stated that he found in the Frankfurt Declaration a "profound lack of Christian politeness," because no attempt had been made to discuss its issues with the Geneva staff. Potter did not mention, however, that the same issues had been voiced in vain by evangelicals at the Uppsala meeting, and that these issues had been published six months prior to the appearance of the Frankfurt Declaration in the book which has already been mentioned, *Humanizierung—Emziger—der Welt?* (later appearing in English as *Missions: Which Way?*) Above all, Potter did not reveal that the Theological Convention, in letters to the General Secretaries of the WCC and of the Lutheran World Federation, had offered to send a delegation to Geneva in order to conduct a responsible, top-level deliberation on the issues of the Frankfurt Declaration. This offer was treated rather dilatorily and finally rejected. A panel discussion staged by the German Missionary Council in September 1970 in Berlin, in which Potter, Hollenweger and also two authors of the Frankfurt Declaration participated, was far too short to lead to any results, and could, therefore, never be accepted as a substitute for the responsible consultation we had requested.

Readers of the World Council's official ecumenical periodicals and press service never had the opportunity to read the Frankfurt Declaration, unless they had obtained it through other sources. In an age where "dialogue" has been all but idolized, dialogue was denied to concerned theological scholars who sincerely sought for it. Moslems, Buddhists, Marxists, and men of other religions and ideologies have been more fortunate in ecumenical treatment.

I must add in all fairness, however, that the CWME has invited me to attend its forthcoming World Conference

72

at Bangkok. I have accepted this invitation. I hope that the conference theme, "Salvation Today," will offer the opportunity to voice the concerns of the Frankfurt Declaration. I confess that I am not optimistic. These theological principles will most likely be bogged down in the swamp of ecumenical pluralism. Therefore we still hold to the necessity of urging a responsible confrontation over the content of the Frankfurt Declaration itself, where both sides are equally represented.

WHAT LIES AHEAD?

Has the Frankfurt Declaration, like other contemporary statements, run its course? Are not new issues coming up which demand new approaches and answers? Although it is a bit awkward to appear to plead one's own case, I definitely think that the Frankfurt Declaration has a continuing function.

Even at the time of this writing, the Frankfurt Declaration had once more been the focus of some very significant developments both in Germany and overseas. I recently received a letter from Bandung stating that the Frankfurt Declaration has just been sent out to 2,000 Indonesian clergymen and missionaries. The churches in Indonesia up to now have been quite homogenously orthodox in their reformed theology, but the Indonesian Council of Churches has developed more of an evangelistic concern in view of the unique ingatherings during the past seven years. But today they are also adversely affected by the ecumenical ferment. The Ecumenical Institute of Chicago in its Singapore outpost is working hard to speed up this process. The Bangkok "Salvation Today" meeting is also casting its shadows ahead. Some concerned evangelical theologians in Bandung felt that Indonesian Christians should see the new ideological conflicts threatening the life and mission of the Church. They regarded the Frankfurt Declaration a most helpful tool to arouse the theological conscience of Indonesian church leaders.

Another most heartening development took place in Germany itself in February, 1972. The general crisis in German missions has been sharpening. Attempts of the leaders of the Geneva-linked German Missionary Council to bring about a new theological consensus among its members have only resulted in a clearer apprehension of the theological disunity of the Council. The recent ecumenical program of combating racism has deeply shaken the remaining confidence of some evangelical societies still in the Geneva orbit. Thus the German Conference of Evangelical Missions has decided to strengthen its position by adopting the Frankfurt Declaration as a statement containing its own understanding of mission. This was done with the understanding that within the Conference several views of the Church and its sacraments are represented, and that consent given to the Frankfurt Declaration does not imply the adoption of one particular point of view on the secondary issues.

It seems to me that the German Conference of Evangelical Missions has found the solution to an internal denominational difficulty which could well serve as a model for evangelical missionary societies around the world. The Frankfurt Declaration, side by side with the Wheaton Declaration, could become a rallying point for closer fellowship on the basis of a common concept of mission. The Frankfurt Declaration might promote an even wider fellowship with those Christians who do not call themselves evangelicals, but who in all basic concerns are evangelical in their hearts.

Obviously, mere formalistic assent to the Frankfurt Declaration will not be enough. The document must not become a fetish. In at least two ways the spirit of the Frankfurt Declaration can be broadened and deepened in the days to come.

1. Many people have asked for a more popular version. Something is needed to convey these missionary convictions to Christians who do not have the theological training necessary to recognize the heresies the Frankfurt Declaration refutes. The Frankfurt Theological Convention has already produced a preliminary draft of a popular version. When matured, it will be available for distribution in German-speaking congregations. Perhaps the same thing could be done for churches speaking other languages.

2. A number of important theological issues are only briefly touched in the Frankfurt Declaration. They need further clarification. I am thinking, for example, about the relation between verbal witness and social service

as two sides of the total mission of the Church. Then too, in Asia, theologians wanted to go deeper into the significance of Eastern religions in the light of biblical revelation.

Missiologists all over the world, who are in basic agreement with the Frankfurt and Wheaton Declarations, should go more deeply into such issues and communicate their findings to each other. An effective missionary strategy cannot be confined solely to practical methods. It should be based upon a solid doctrinal foundation. Hopefully the Frankfurt and Wheaton Declarations can be used at least as a starting point for such a new, worldwide venture in missiology.

6

Opportunities and Dangers in Asia

Up to this point this book has dealt largely with the contemporary developments of the theology of mission in Germany and the Western nations in general. While it would be well to include chapters on all three Third World continents, my first-hand data is still incomplete on Africa and Latin America. Therefore I am limited to Asia only.

Last year I was privileged to undertake a rather extensive lecture tour through the Far East. This presented the opportunity for personal and direct orientation to the present spiritual situation in churches in Japan, Hong Kong, Taiwan, New Guinea, Singapore, and Indonesia. In trying to summarize the bewildering multitude of impressions received during this journey, three general categories stand out: opportunities, threats, and responsibilities.

TODAY'S OPPORTUNITIES IN ASIA

Visiting sister churches in Asia is an experience which one does not easily forget. First of all (in spite of many signs of alarm) it is a most encouraging experience. One is excited to find that most congregations in Asia are alive, that new ways of witness and service are being discovered, and that new doors are opening for evangelism. The churches and congregations in Asian countries differ greatly in size. The congregations of Japan to which I preached numbered only 50 on the average and some were even smaller, despite twenty years of hard, evangelistic work. In Indonesia I preached to overcrowded churches in Sumatra and Kalimantan, attended by 500 or more. I was thrilled by the joy and vitality radiating from most of these congregations. In the congregations gathered by individual soul-winning, this was the joy of new-found liberty and meaning in life. In the larger churches, formed through people movements, it was the confident assurance that Christ had established His reign over this particular people, and that He had made them His own royal nation. Out of the many quarreling "margas" (the Batak or rather Sanskrit name for clan) Christ had formed one Church - His new marga, transcending former feuds and value systems.

In the Toba-Batak Church of Pematang Sienter, I witnessed a tremendous response when I applied I Peter 2:9, "But you are a chosen race, a royal priesthood, a holy nation, a people of His acquisition, so that you may proclaim the perfections of Him who called you out of darkness into His marvelous light." I felt that they needed this reminder since these Indonesian people-movement Churches, in their self-assured mentality are so much like the German tribal Churches of medieval times!

All these churches readily listened to a biblically-based message. Christians sing their new praise with great joy and are ready to serve their congregations in deep, personal dedication. Most of the Churches in Asia have been founded and enlarged by spontaneous witnessing, and the pastoral responsibility has fallen to active lay leaders.

What encouraged me most was the youth of the Asian congregations. The average age in all was low. Some congregations have instituted special youth services in order to accommodate all their members in Sunday worship. About fifty per cent of the total Asian population is under twenty-five, and the average age in the younger Churches reflects the demographic situation.

An elderly German colleague of mine once entitled a book: *The Riches of Asia, Her Christians.* If I had time, I would like to write a similar book called *The Riches of Asia, Her Young Christians.* This thrilling observation is bolstered by the fact that all Asian countries have most energetic evangelical student movements. My visit to Japan was initiated by one of these, the KGK, the Evangelical University Movement of that country. The KGK consists mainly of students who have personally been won to Christ from Shintoism and Buddhism through fellow students. By means of regular annual Bible camps, new converts are made. and many volunteer for active evangelistic service in Japan as well as for the foreign field. As I understand it, one of the strongest student organizations is to be found in Korea. Because of their thorough grounding in the Scriptures, the members of this group carry on weekly Bible studies without need of assistance from the professional clergy.

A significant indication of the winds of change blowing over the world-wide Church is the appointment of a Chinese Christian, Chua Wee Hian, as the new General Secretary of the International Federation of Evangelical Students.

NEW DOORS OF WITNESS

The Churches in Asia are very conscious of changing historical situations and the new socio-political reality in which they live. They are eager to discover new doors of witness through which they can carry the Gospel into the non-Christian environment and prove that it has meaning for our modern way of life.

I saw, for example, successful attempts to plant new churches or cells in the fast-growing urban settlements which shoot up like mushrooms in the industrial areas. In Japan, kindergartens or English courses provide the first points of contact. They create opportunities to meet the people and to communicate the Gospel to them. Soon a little flock of inquirers forms the nucleus of a future congregation.

Another experiment in Tokyo involves pastoral counseling by telephone. The commercial boom of Japanese industrial production creates a permanent stress situation, driving many people to despair. The challenge to volunteer for this new service was taken up immediately by hundreds of Christians who are now engaged in throwing out the telephone "life-line" to people engulfed by seemingly impossible situations, some of whom are on the brink of suicide.

I was further impressed by the excellent use which evangelical missions in Asia are making of radio evangelism. This provides a welcome opportunity for interdenominational cooperation. I found that the radio programs in general are geared to the varying interests of the listeners. The large listener correspondence and the many who take Bible correspondence courses prove that the net is not cast out in vain. Both direct and indirect forms of approach have their effect. Every morning at 6:20, for example, Lutheran evangelist Masaki gives his straightforward Gospel message. Thousands of Christian and non-Christian students, waiting for the English course at 6:30, listen to him. Mrs. Masaki has a full-time job replying to all the letters which come in as a result of her husband's radio ministry.

EVANGELISTIC OPENINGS

This goes to prove that the churches in Asia, in spite of many obstacles, still find open doors for preaching the Gospel to the non-Christian world. Asia as a whole may not be a ripe harvest field at the present time, but in every country certain units of society for the first time have really opened up to the Christian message. Newly-discovered tribes in the highlands of West Irian, still living in cannibalism only a dozen years ago, have been reached by pioneer missionaries. Tens of thousands have been baptized and formed into congregations.

In recent years the most fertile fields in Asia have been some of the Indonesian islands, especially East Java, Timor, and northern Sumatra. A providential coincidence of spiritual and political factors brought this about. The cruel backlash to the attempted communist take-over had shaken the socio-religious foundations of the nation. At the same time the Spirit of God was raising up powerful evangelists, eager to sow the fast-sprouting seed of the

Gospel. The problem was how the great harvest could be brought in, and how so many newly-established congregations could receive a thorough grounding in Christian doctrine and morals.

I cannot forget my meeting with the leaders of the Indonesian Missionary Fellowship, an offshoot of the World-wide Evangelization Crusade in East Java. They had established a Bible school which every year sends out dozens of evangelistic teams to carry the fire-brand of the Gospel to all Indonesian islands and also to other Asian countries as far away as Pakistan. "To us," Rev. Scheunemann, one of these leaders, declared, "it appears like an evening wind of the Holy Spirit which gives quite new and unexpected opportunities to the Gospel."

I must confess that when I hear that some of the last countries to remain closed to Christian missions, such as Nepal, Afghanistan and even Yemen are opening up for the first time, I wonder whether the literal fulfillment of Christ's prophecy in Matthew 24:14 is occurring: "And this good news of the kingdom will be preached all over the world to testify to all the nations, and then the end will come."

THREATS FROM THE ANTICHRIST

The preaching of the Gospel to all nations is the positive sign through which the Lord teaches us to recognize the approaching end of present history. But in the same connection He also tells which negative signs will precede His second coming. These include the persecution of the Church and the appearance of false prophets and false Christs. While persecution constitutes a menace to the Church from the outside, the activity of lying prophets and antichrists is a danger which arises from the inside.

I do not want to say much about the persecution of the Asian Church. It is enough to note that in the largest of all Asian countries, mainland China, the Christian Church is suffering one of the most severe persecutions which any church has had to endure since the beginning of the modern missionary movement. Similar persecution has taken place in northern Korea and northern Viet Nam. Persecution may, indeed, come to Christians in Taiwan if this free part of China is eventually united with the mainland.

Non-Christian religions are becoming stronger in all Eastern countries and new syncretistic religions are arising to capture the loyalty of millions. The "new religions in Japan," for example, have had extraordinary growth since World War II. They promise a satisfying, liberating, beneficent life-force to their 20 million adherents. They all bear messianic features and each claims it will become the future universal religion for all of mankind. Up to now they maintain an outward attitude of tolerance, but if someday they manage to become allied with certain political powers, things might become rather difficult for Christianity.

At the present time, however, I am much more concerned about the insidious spiritual paralysis which has stricken many Christian workers both in missions and indigenous churches. This easily quenches the apostolic spirit of many missionaries, pastors and church leaders.

Much has been written recently about the crisis in missions, and many missiologists have attempted to find a remedy. Usually the crisis has been blamed on the changed historical situation in the post-colonial era. The slogan "missionary go home," is now used as a watchword for the ecumenical concept of mission.

Here the old one-way traffic of missionaries to far-off lands is replaced by inter-church relations between a Western church and an autonomous church in Asia which, generally speaking, can manage its own affairs.

A steady stream of missionaries return home because they feel they are not wanted any more. To a point they are forced home because the Western missionary societies can no longer support them. When the American representative of the Interboard Committee which channels the joint assistance program of seven American churches to the United Church of Christ in Japan, arrived in Tokyo in April of 1971, he opened his speech with the following remark: "Last year I came as an apostle of gloom. I am afraid this year things have not become brighter." The reason for this financial recess is obviously the crisis of faith which has befallen many large denominations in the West. Even the Missouri Synod Lutherans are facing such a crisis, and are forced to cut down the number of missionaries they send.

In addition to the economic problem, many missionaries have been shaken by the spread of new concepts such as the theology of secularization. I observed this in all major Protestant denominations as well as in the Roman Catholic Church. When I asked an Irish nun, head of a large mission school, about their evangelistic responsibility for Japanese Buddhists and Shintoists, she made the following statement:

> Formerly we took the great commission quite literally, and also the remark attached to it: "he who believes and is baptized will be saved. . ." But since the Second Vatican Council, many once infallible doctrines have become questionable. We no longer have the courage to persuade non-Christians to believe in them. We now only can hope that our silent service will be a witness to our students. [1]

The consequence of such theological relativism is the new readiness for religious coexistence and cooperation. In some denominations, for example, at funerals, Christian and Buddhist rites are often performed side by side.

By far the most radical threat to the life and mission of the Church in Asia is the infiltration of modernist theology. It leads to a watering-down of biblical teaching, and also to a growing polarization. We find in the East Asian countries a definite separation between the conservative-evangelical and the conciliar camps. But even within the ecumenically-oriented churches a group of believers is attempting to remain loyal to the heritage of the Reformation and to soul-winning evangelism.

These churches and missions are caught in the crossfire of invasions from three sides: First is the growing influence of the neo-rationalistic theology of Bultmann, Tillich and others. Their chief exporters are German and American missionaries, reinforced by Asian students who return from studies in overseas theological seminaries.

In Japan a certain missionary told me that his mission board only sends out adherents to modern ecumenical theology. It broadcasts this theology at conferences for missionaries on furlough and through official letters. Any protest against this strategy is condemned as a despicable attempt to bring about schism.

Even more comprehensive are the efforts of the World Council of Churches and now the Lutheran World Federation to impose on all Asian churches Geneva-oriented theology as the dominant doctrine. The two main features of this ecumenical program are the alliance with revolutionary movements in the fight for social justice and the attempt to promote a synthesis with other religions and ideologies as the way toward the unity of all mankind. In New Guinea I found the bishops of the United and Anglican Churches highly disturbed. Geneva had called two revolutionary politicians from New Guinea to attend an ecumenical conference of experts in development in Toyko, in spite of the fact that these two men had openly renounced their church membership by word and deed. Geneva's message claimed that these participants had spoken as representatives of their churches!

THE ECUMENICAL INSTITUTE

But even such procedure is surpassed in its shrewdness by the strategy and methods of the Ecumenical Institute of Chicago. Outwardly this is an instrument of study and consultation. In reality, however, it works like a mission society with the sole purpose of infiltrating the younger churches of Asia and Africa with ultra-modernist theology. It attempts to reeducate churchmen so they will become bridgeheads of revolutionary renewal in their churches.

The ideological foundation of this activity is the proposition that the world has come of age. To meet its claims, men like Bultmann, Tillich, and Niebuhr have engineered a revolution in theology. They have eliminated all metaphysical elements of Bible and theology for which —they say—there is no room in our scientific orientation. All credal statements have to be reinterpreted. The net result is an existential humanism within the framework of a revolutionary philosophy of history. God becomes nothing more than a description of the existential response to a secret impulse from the center of life. The historical person of Jesus Christ is transformed into an abstract "Christ-event." He becomes the "die-and-live Word," an example for us all to die to our own illusions and anxieties and to feel integrated into the universe. By this kind of a new birth people are supposed to be freed from their self-centeredness and thus enabled to dedicate themselves to the service of society. This also becomes the only legitimate model for the renewed Church of the future. It forms the ideological infrastructure for the concept of the "Church for others."

These hollow ideas are stamped into the minds of people through lectures, group discussions, and devotional exercises. The participants in some of the concentrated courses are awakened at daybreak for their first existentialist meditation. Even during table conversations they are obliged to discuss the themes treated in the lectures. The result very often approaches brain-washing. Participants return thoroughly transformed. In their congregations and denominations they then become the multipliers of these ecumenical theories.

The Ecumenical Institute of Chicago develops an effective outreach partially supported by the social activities of a semi-monastic community. Centers are located in the U.S.A., Africa, and Southeast Asia. Influential friends are found in leadership in the larger denominations. Strangely enough, even some Roman Catholic bishops are lending a helping hand.

Nowhere is the worst of these current ecumenical movements revealed so vividly as in this dynamic Institute—this new style missionary society. It aims at nothing less than replacing the biblical nerve center of the churches in Asia and Africa with a pseudo-Christian revolutionary activism. True, at present the leaders of the World Council say they feel rather embarrassed by the Chicago Institute, which has no direct official links with Geneva. But in the deepest analysis, the doctrines of the Institute bear a close resemblance to those characteristic of most of the recent documents of the DWME since New Delhi 1961. In preparation for the world conference which will meet at the end of 1972 in Bangkok, the World Council is offering this same ideology under the label "Salvation Today." To the degree that sound biblical theology melts away, churches become more ready to accept these new ideas being thrust upon them by the

Ecumenical Institute and the Division of World Mission and Evangelism. Churches sleep on, believing that they are remaining faithful to the "convictions of our fathers interpreted in modern day terms." The reality, of course, is that biblical convictions have been destroyed by the interpretation.

EVANGELICAL RESPONSIBILITY

We have seen what unusual evangelistic opportunities the Asian countries present today. We have also been warned of the theological crisis which threatens to undermine the witness of the Asian churches. Now we turn to the challenge. How can we avoid the danger of losing our opportunities in this decisive hour?

First we must differentiate between the various kinds of churches and missions operating in Asia today. One group, because of strong ties to the neo-liberal forces in the West, has fully adopted the ecumenical line. Quite a number of mission societies belong to this group. Among the Asian churches I would mention the Protestant Kyodan in Japan and the Presbyterian Church in Taiwan, although the latter left the World Council for political reasons.

Another, much larger, group has just begun to be infiltrated by modernistic currents. I include most of the confessional churches and missions in this category: Anglicans, Lutherans, Presbyterians, and others.

The third group includes the spectrum of churches allied with Western conservative-evangelicals. Ecclesiastical divisions in Asia reflect almost exactly the situation within Western Christianity. In view of the spiritual battle now being waged in Germany, I was consoled by I Peter 5:9: "Firm in your faith, resist him, aware that throughout the world, sufferings of this kind are imposed upon your brothers."

I am convinced that our main challenge today consists of strengthening this world-wide brotherhood of *martyria* by which I mean biblical and evangelical witness.

What might this mean in practice? As to the first group of missions and churches sailing the good ship *Oikumene* we should do all we can to challenge their smug assumption that they have the only right position. We should encourage

85

our conservative brethren in Asia, fearing nothing, to seek opportunities for a theological encounter. In spiritual warfare, the best defense lies in attack.

As to the second group, our main task is to inform them of the smouldering conflicts. In their isolation many sincere church workers exhibit a theological credulity which makes them easy prey for camouflaged modernism. We should stretch out our hands in support of all evangelical-minded Christians within these churches who do their best to keep the faith.

The main responsibility of fulfilling the unfinished task of evangelizing Asia falls increasingly upon the shoulders of the conservative-evangelicals. They preserve the strongest sense of evangelistic vocation. They muster the largest number of missionaries, and they structure their church-mission relationships so as not to eliminate all foreign missionaries. They rightly see that evangelistic and church-planting missionaries are still much needed.

EVANGELICAL PROBLEM AREAS

The evangelical churches and missions have their weaknesses. I am convinced that unless they overcome these they will not be in a strong position to meet the challenge of increased responsibility. What are these problem areas?

1. Evangelicals should strive for greater visible unity. Maps of evangelical forces distributed in Asian countries often give a rather chaotic impression. The Wheaton Declaration rightly says: "Evangelicals have not fully manifested this biblical oneness because of carnal differences and personal grievances—and thus missionary advance has been hindered." [2]

2. Evangelicals ought to give more emphasis to theological studies. They need to be able to analyze the present innocent-sounding deviations in their anti-Christian depth. They must resist the enemy by force of superior biblical arguments. I have found that the apologetic content of the Frankfurt Declaration has not really been grasped by many evangelicals in Asia. They were not aware of the issues at stake, issues which threaten their own existence. The emphasis on revival and evangelism, important as it is,

86

must not prevent us from paying due attention to doctrine and apologetics. I, therefore, strongly support the Theological Assistance Program for Asia, which is making an increasingly helpful contribution. Graduate studies in theology and missions for missionaries on furlough are also very helpful.

3. Evangelicals ought to develop a deeper appreciation of the biblical reality of the visible Church. In their concern for the genuineness of evangelism, regeneration, and personal holiness, evangelicals have often bypassed the necessary corporate fruit of Christian mission, namely the fully-organized responsible church. This causes lack of unity and coordination among evangelical groups. This shortcoming also hinders the application of elementary church growth principles, pointed out so masterfully by Donald McGavran and his fellow scholars. Thus, despite increase of foreign workers, evangelical faith missions cannot show corresponding numerical fruit. Here evangelicals would do well to pay more attention to writings coming out of the Institute of Church Growth in Pasadena, as well as the findings of the Green Lake Conference, published under the title, *Church/Mission Tensions Today.*[3]

The battle cry in our crucial situation in Asia today should be: "Let all positive forces be mustered to meet the joint missionary and apologetic challenge."

BRIDGEHEADS FOR EVANGELICALS

Some bridgeheads for such an evangelical gathering already exist in Asia. In most cases, their objectives are simply devotional. Perhaps a strong impulse from the outside may help in creating a new awareness for needed cooperation.

It has recently been suggested that Billy Graham's forthcoming World Congress on Evangelization may become the rallying point for evangelical missionary forces.

To conclude this chapter, I would like to point up two considerations for a possible missionary fellowship which would extend not only to Asia, but to other parts of the world. In the first place, any evangelical missionary fellowship needs a sound doctrinal basis, relevant to contemporary issues. A statement like the Frankfurt Declaration could be helpful here.

In the second place, bridges should be built between different kinds of evangelicals. Those represented by the Evangelical Foreign Missions Association and the Interdenominational Foreign Mission Association have already established productive relationships. But a further step is needed. This would involve fellowship between those who have separated from conciliar denominations and those evangelicals who have chosen to remain within. Perhaps we should try to give the term "evangelical" a wider interpretation which would include, for example, Lutheran pietism. According to my conviction, all Christians earn the name "evangelical" who are faithful to the authority and unity of the Bible, who share concerns for spiritual life, revival, and evangelism, and who defend the purity and vitality of the Gospel against modernism and false ecumenism.

This opens up some new possibilities for interdenominational fellowship in mission. On my Asian journey I have learned that the real frontiers of faith and witness cut across the traditional denominational lines. We would do well to heed the signs of the times and encourage each other as evangelical believers worldwide. By doing this we will be able more effectively to meet the challenge for winning Asia, as well as other parts of the world, for Christ.

7

Missions and Racism

In September, 1970, the Executive Committee of the World Council of Churches adopted a new program designed to combat racism. This touched off hectic arguments among Christians all over the world as to whether the Church should be involved with the forces of violent revolution. No matter which side we stand on, one thing is sure: simple protests against racism are not enough. Christians whose consciences are bound by the Scripture are forced to give their own answers as to how the racial issue should be understood in the context of the Gospel of peace.

RACISM AS SIN

To begin with, we should attempt a definition of racism. The following may be helpful: racism is the theoretical and practical inclination to overstate the values and privileges of one's own race at the expense of the dignity of people of other races and of fellowship with them.

There are, of course, differing degrees of racism, starting with hidden emotional feelings and ending with brutal political programs of extinction. Thus we must avoid making generalizations. Racism, as a personal or collective attitude, is caused by one's own feelings or interests, but it is often rationalized on ideological grounds.

Philosophical, religious, and even biblical grounds are mentioned. People often speak of the historic mission of their own race as preserving or spreading the values of that particular culture. Negatively, some declare that other races are less gifted in respect to intellect, culture, and character. The genetic heritage of some is even considered to be deficient. Racists feel obliged to maintain the purity of their own race, subjugating all other races.

In the deepest theological analysis, racism is rooted in man's original sin. This is manifested in pride and selfishness as well as in fear and delusion. Christians cannot be indifferent to the implications of all of this. They must be profoundly moved by any appearance of racism, since its inhuman effects contradict the message entrusted to them by God.

EVIL EFFECTS OF RACISM

Racism has caused untold harm and suffering among men. The tragedy is that the people who were most affected were those to whom modern Christian missions directed their efforts. True enough, racism is not confined to white people. But unquestionably, it has occurred among whites to a special degree and on a wide scale. The African peoples have suffered particular harm at the hands of the white man. Americans extracted them as slaves. Europeans dominated their land politically and supressed the black people on their own soil. Today southern Africa stands out as an area where the non-white people are deprived of many elementary rights. In the U.S.A. formal law does grant civil rights to the blacks, but especially in the southern states these rights are still met by tenacious resistance. The peoples affected by racism are injured mentally and physically. Their reaction becomes even more bitter when they are aware that racism is so contrary to the Christian faith which is professed by many of the white oppressors.

CHRISTIAN INVOLVEMENT IN RACISM

The scandalous contrast between racism and Christianity is accentuated by another regrettable phenomenon: the

Christian Church and to a point even Christian missions are guilty of tolerating the development of racism.

It can be proved that in South Africa the ideology of apartheid originated from the churches' application of racial segregation to their European and non-European constituency. Even today most white congregations in South Africa would not allow a black person to partake in their worship service.

The situation in the U.S.A. appears almost as bad. Black evangelist Tom Skinner has entitled one of the chapters of his autobiography, "Where Do They Fail?" In his shocking statement, he relentlessly castigates the attitude of conservative evangelicals whose pride in biblical orthodoxy stands in a strange contrast to their unconcern for the misery in the black ghettos.

> This individual had a half dozen Bible quotations for every social problem that existed. . . If you told him about the conditions in Harlem, he would cry out with typical piety "Christ is the answer!" He considered himself one of the last group really holding on to the fundamental truth. But he was choking on that fundamental truth. He should have taken that truth out into the main stream of everyday life and made Jesus Christ relevant to the drug addict, the alcoholic, that individual who is down and out . . . To the shame of so-called white evangelical Christianity in this country they have neglected one of the most significant, one of the most fruitful mission fields in the world —the American Negro. [1]

PARALYSIS OF THE EVANGELISTIC WITNESS

The failure of many missions to relate properly to the racial question has obstructed their witness. Are we still surprised that many peoples have turned a deaf ear to mission societies that have remained indifferent to the sin of racism? In many districts of Africa, especially in the cities, the Christian message is ceasing to produce real fruit. Many Africans regard white missionaries and also their black fellow-workers simply as religious exponents of the oppressive white system. In South Africa, racism has been the principal cause of so many African

Christians leaving their churches in order to establish independent separatist movements. This is paralleled in the U.S.A. by the multiplication of Negro sects including the Black Muslim movement. Deep schisms have occurred which seemingly will never be healed.

THE BIBLICAL TEACHING ON RACISM

The biblical teaching on racism cannot be handled in a superficial manner by quoting a few rather handy proof-texts. The issue must rather be developed in light of the biblical history of creation and redemption. I shall attempt this by enunciating four biblical propositions.

1. The Bible affirms the unity and diversity of mankind. Owing to their common origin, all men are by nature one.

Human history begins with the creation of man in the image of God. God has destined man to live in fellowship both with his Creator and also with fellow humans. The first chapter of the Bible points up the diversity of the human race. God created male and female. This sexual differentiation is not designed to produce separation and opposition, but fellowship and mutual assistance. Man and woman complement each other and this diversity contains no hint of discrimination. Each has equal value, each is made in God's image. This means that all additional human differences, whether biological, psychological, cultural, or social are of secondary importance in contrast to the essential destiny of man: to live as God's own image and in social fellowship.

But this original harmony has been disturbed by the fall. Because of the disobedience of our first parents, humanity as a whole has been separated from God (Romans 5:12-14). And as a result even personal and social relations between man are corrupted.

This social breakdown began with man and wife. After the fall, God said to the woman: "I will greatly increase your pregnancy-troubles; you will suffer birth-pangs; yet, you will be drawn to your husband and he will dominate you" (Gen. 3:16). This punishment constitutes a clear relation of subordination which is marked by suffering.

A few chapters later we hear of another social effect

of the fall, this time within the larger human family. Ham shamelessly offends the respectability of his father Noah. His brothers try to make amends, but Noah curses, in the person of Canaan, the descendants of Ham: "Cursed be Canaan! May he be a servant of servants to his brothers." He then added, "Blessed be the Lord, the God of Shem and may Canaan be his servant. May God make Japheth so great that he shall dwell in Shem's tents; and may Canaan be their servant" (Gen. 9:25-27). Here for the first time in biblical history we catch a glimpse of the riddle of racial antagonism, conditioned by an original curse, evoked by an original sin.

Then in the eleventh chapter of the same book of Genesis we read the story of human presumptuousness. Mankind tries to construct a united megapolis and a tower. This gives expression to the rebellious desire of man without God to be like God. But God confounds this plan. He condemns mankind to live in ethnic groups, each with its own social and political order. He also confuses their languages, thus preventing mankind from developing a common, universal culture. From here on, human creativity develops along diverse cultural lines. This separation of man from man is at once a divine punishment and divine mercy. It will finally be overcome in the eschatological kingdom. But for the time being the history of mankind is national and ethnic history. God acts through nations and peoples.

Thus humanity as we know it is separated in two dimensions. Vertically, man is separated from God. Horizontally, men are separated from each other. God has provided an order of preservation upheld by ethical commandments common to all men. But mankind is also diversified by boundaries, customs, and languages—all integral parts of God's plan in history.

2. Jesus Christ constitutes a new community out of all races.

But now, in the fulness of time (Gal. 4:4), a new beginning in the history of mankind has been made. God Himself in the person of His Son has come as man. This is Jesus Christ, the new man, the second Adam, in whom a new united humanity begins.

As the Son, He is also the true image of God, in whom man fulfills his own destiny. As the servant of God, Christ dies the atoning death on the cross, removing the curse of our sin. Thus the relationships of man to God and man to man are restored. That which separated us from each other has now been removed by grace. Freely we may approach God and each other. "Which is that God was in Christ reconciling the world to Himself, not counting up their sins against them, and committing to us the message of reconciliation" (2 Cor. 5:19). This work of reconciliation was done once for all and on behalf of the whole world. Nobody is excluded. It is God's will that each man and woman be His child, and that he relate to others as brothers and sisters. All enmity, estrangement, and oppression of men by other men is eliminated. Racism is also removed. Because of Christ's atonement, all distinctions of sex, wealth, race, nationality, culture, and language no longer have the power of separation.

Where God Himself no longer separates, integration of the races has become a possibility. "As many of you as have been baptized into Christ have clothed yourselves with Christ. There is neither Jew nor Greek, there is neither slave nor freeman, there is neither male nor female, because you are all one in Christ Jesus" (Gal. 3:27-28).

But we must be careful at this point. Do these words really imply that since Calvary racial distinctions no longer exist? Does it mean that differences produced by creation and the fall have passed away? This would be an inaccurate understanding of the text. It is not only refuted by stark reality but also by the words of the Bible itself.

The fifth chapter of Second Corinthians verse 17 says: "Accordingly, if any one is in Christ he is a new creation. The old is gone; lo, the new has come." This seemingly little phrase "in Christ" (which also appears in our other quote from Galatians, "you are all one in Christ Jesus") is of immense importance for the understanding of our problem. It teaches us two things:

First it teaches us that Christ's work of reconciliation is not directly related to the political and social orders. Neither Christ nor the apostles attempted to dissolve the social order of their time. What we do have in Christ is the reconciling effect of His love so that we can live in a new fellowship with God and with other men.

In the second place, the phrase "in Christ" implies that the new fellowship is not produced in human history automatically. Rather this reconciliation, sufficient for all, becomes fully effective only in those people who permit themselves to be reconciled to God and to each other.

Outside this new realm, indicated by the phrase "in Christ," the old separations, both vertical and horizontal, are still in effect. They will not be removed as long as this world still lies under Satan's rule.

In other words, while we as Christians may maintain that racial brotherhood is possible, we do not expand it to a general political truth. World conditions today would tend to falsify such a statement, even if it is meant only as a future aim. Our affirmation of racial brotherhood is valid only in conjunction with the phrase "in Christ." This places us within the realm of life of the Christian Church. We have no way to enforce the integration of nations, races, and classes who hate each other. Neither a clever political program nor even the power of arms would do. All such attempts are rightly judged by this remark of Tom Skinner:

> But the riots, the disturbances, the intense bigotry
> and racism in America proved that men are not
> basically good but rather basically sinful and that
> it takes the regeneration from Jesus Christ alone
> to change society. [2]

3. The Church is able to work for racial reconciliation even beyond its own circle.

Does this mean that any attempts to find a political and social solution to the racial problem are doomed to failure until all involved have become regenerated Christians? If we interpret the New Testament message of reconciliation in such exclusive terms, we have again misunderstood it. In that case the risen Christ would rule only in pious convents (And even they do not always exhibit perfect brotherliness!). But Jesus not only calls His disciples to be the little flock persecuted in the world; He also calls them to be the salt of the earth and the light of the world. He compares the Kingdom of God in history with leaven.

Even though a minority, a church which testifies to Christ by word and deed can bring about change in the total life of the larger community. By projecting new ideals derived from the Gospel, it can help other people abandon their inhuman behavior.

I could even go one step further and venture the following statement: Whenever such a representative Christian community proclaims the total Lordship of Christ by word and deed, Satan is already partially dethroned as are the powers of separation.

I believe that in the past Europeans and Americans have experienced these leavening effects of the Gospel. They have caused them to write constitutions which were at least basically in agreement with the biblical commandments which explicitly refer to the reign of God.

Because Christ is the Lord over both church and world, the lifegiving and renewing forces which are "in Christ" have their effect to a limited extent on the whole social realm in which the true Church witnesses. This shows that in order to improve the social order of this world, our Lord needs a strong Church everywhere, a Church strong in membership, but above all strong in faith and obedience.

4. Only the Lord Himself at His second coming will establish the multi-racial community.

To complete our understanding of racial problems in the context of biblical history, one more clarification needs to be made. The Word of God does not promise that the Gospel will be received equally by all nations. Christian mission acts under the injunction to preach the Gospel of the Kingdom as a witness to all nations.

But if a nation does not obey, the same witness may also be turned against it on the judgment day. We must also take into account the tempting power of Satan. The New Testament clearly predicts that toward the end of history mankind will pass through the reign of the Antichrist. The forces of evil will be loosed to an unprecedented extent. This will in turn cause a new outbreak of racism which will end in a mutual slaughtering of the nations. Only Jesus Christ will put an end to this when He comes to establish His universal Kingdom of peace. This means that racism will finally be overcome not by us, nor even by the preaching of the Gospel, but only by the Lord Himself when He returns to fulfill His eschatological promises.

This eschatological outlook is not intended to discourage our present efforts to be peacemakers. It rather encourages them. For in establishing signs of peace here and now, we anticipate by faith the presence of the Lord, who will come to reward these efforts in His own Kingdom.

WHAT MISSIONS CAN DO

One thing is clear from Scripture: If there is any power in the world which can overcome racism, it is the Gospel.

If this is true, why have our churches achieved so little? What should Christian missions do to avoid becoming caricatures of evangelical Christianity as authors, such as Tom Skinner, have suggested? There is one basic answer. If the Gospel is not to be rejected as simply hollow words, we must take steps to make it relevant as an experiential reality in the midst of racial tensions.

What does this mean in practice?

UNVEILING THE SIN

As the power of the Gospel can only be experienced by repentant sinners, the first step is to unveil the sinful causes of racism in our own lives and ask forgiveness for them.

When European people discuss the racial conflict in other parts of the world, they tend to exhibit a spirit of irritation and judgment. They profess their inability to understand the inhuman behavior of the whites in those racist countries. But quite often these same people do an about face when they become personally involved in areas of racial tension. This happens particularly if they have settled and developed a vested interest in such countries. This helps us recognize the fact that in social matters our judgment is often biased. By nature we are inclined to regard our own interests as more important than those of our fellow men. We unconsciously form our theories in the light of our own desires and anxieties, without seeing life's circumstances through the eyes of our brother. The real motives behind our theories are often self-preservation, ambition, craving for possession and pleasure, or the anxiety of our guilty conscience.

All this stems from the original human attitude of selfishness. It prevents us from having genuine fellowship with our neighbor. Racism is just one of the many expressions of the selfishness which directs our aggressions to those of other races. And if we do not have any racist feelings it may just be due to the lack of opportunity because of geographical or social accidents. But in those cases, racism is often substituted by professional arrogance, autocratic behavior, rivalism, denominationalism, or nationalism. All these attitudes are analogous to racism. They add a sinful dimension to our own social relations.

It is absurd, therefore, to try to overcome racism with an exaggerated spirit of anti-racism. Militant anti-racism can only intensify the racism of our opponents, and in a sense make us reverse racists. We can only be of help to racists if we can suggest a remedy against racism which we have experienced in our own lives. As Christians we should be well aware of it. It is nothing less than the Gospel, which assures us that our hostility toward God and toward our own fellow men has been overcome by Jesus Christ.

THE GOSPEL OF RECONCILIATION

Christian mission can overcome racism by applying the Gospel to racists and to their victims as the model for their reconciliation.

Every person who understands the depth of the racial conflicts in Southern Africa and in the U.S.A., knows that the real problem is not in the area of objective solutions. It is rather the hardening of *attitudes* on both sides of the color bar. Any proposed solution is met by distrust and intuitive opposition. Here is where church and mission have their greatest opportunity to contribute to solving the political dilemma. Christians know how deeply sin is rooted in their own human natures. They also know the power of the Gospel to change hearts. Experience has shown that human attitudes can be changed for the better, both in individuals and in groups.

As missionaries we are obligated to expose the sinful

presuppositions on both sides which frustrate reconciliation. In South Africa, for example, we must expose the drive for self-preservation, motivated by fear of the collective extinction of whites. Behind this lies deep-seated guilt feelings. But such fear can be overcome by a new self-surrender to the sovereignty and mercy of God. This produces a new love for the injured brother. The path toward this goal leads through the forgiveness of sins.

The deepest wounds to the African victims of white racism have been inflicted by the persistent insults to their human dignity. This has produced hatred and bitterness. The blacks are frustrated in their struggle for a higher social status. The Gospel speaks to us again here. It tells us that our real dignity and status are not ultimately dependent upon the recognition of man. Jesus has elevated us to the highest dignity conceivable by making us sons of God Himself.

I am not proposing that changing hearts is an alternative to changing unjust social structures. But the change of hearts is the strongest incentive I know to encourage people to change unjust social structures and to avoid the common problem of abusing the new social structures once they are in power. Furthermore, when hearts are changed and lives transformed, human relations in general are more likely to be harmonious, even if the social and political structures cannot be changed at once.

THE POWER OF PRAYER

Many people suspect prayer to be merely an attempt to escape social responsibility. But if we admit changed hearts pave the way for changing social structures, we also realize that this is a work of the Spirit of God. With respect to Southern Africa, for example, I refuse to give up the hope for a moral awakening within the large Afrikaans-speaking churches, which includes the entire Boer population. If these churches, by a sudden stirring of conscience, would change their ways, South Africa as a nation would be transformed. Should not believers in all parts of the world join together in prayer towards this goal? It could happen.

As we have seen, theologically speaking it is only within the community of the Christian Church that racism can be attacked at its roots. Even within the brotherhood, fellowship is constantly threatened by sin. But the blood of Christ has abundant power to heal such wounds. In this fallen world, the Church is the beginning of the new creation. As such it is the sign of hope for all of mankind still groaning in travail.

Wherever racial tensions exist, therefore, Christian missions ought to demonstrate the reality of inter-racial brotherhood in the churches they plant. I maintain that the Church has a right to speak about the racial issue in society only when it has put things straight inside its own house.

I vividly remember the joy in the congregation at Lobethal in Transvaal in April, 1958. The believers were celebrating the baptism of our son when we were missionaries there. We had chosen not to have him baptized in a European congregation, but rather in the Sotho-speaking service together with a black child of the same village.

THE RIGHTS OF THE OPPRESSED

Since we ourselves have been delivered by the love of God, we can courageously stand for the rights of those who are racially oppressed. The love of Christ is manifested not only within the sheltered walls of the congregation, but it also radiates out. It impels us actively to search for our oppressed fellow men in their emergency situation. It drives us to stand openly and firmly with them for their liberation. This might involve difficulties and even persecutions by state officials. We may be ostracized by the powers that be. But it is a risk we must take.

In South Africa some white churches have begun to regain the confidence of the more politically-conscious black people. It was thought that it could not be done. But when they took the risk of openly defending the rights of the oppressed through public protests and practical assistance, the picture changed. Unfortunately, these are still isolated cases, but they could easily become the norm if the Church had a change of heart.

POLITICAL EFFORTS

The churches should support all sincere efforts made by the government or the opposition to find peaceful solutions to the racial conflicts. They should encourage their members to participate actively in them. It is the aim of mission that God's rule be brought to bear on all spheres of human life. Mission, therefore, must sympathetically support the efforts of political leaders, lawyers, educationalists, and social workers who make an effort to give greater recognition to the human dignity of underprivileged racial groups. This makes it necessary for churches and missions to get a clear picture of the social conditions of their own country. They must make it a point to investigate how far the different reform movements agree with the Christian view of man and his community.

We must admit that the Gospel does not supply us with a detailed strategy as to how, out of a fallen world, we can bring about a totally satisfactory order of society. Naturally, the Church can never wholly identify with a given political movement which attempts to overcome racism. But nevertheless, it should encourage its members to cooperate as fully as possible with any political movement whose aims are noble. The Church must do whatever is necessary to convince its members that applying Christian ethical principles to society should be given highest priority. Every Christian should be concerned with protecting the weak, preserving the family, respecting human dignity and maintaining equality before the law.

An objection will undoubtedly have arisen. Some will have said that all this is far too slow and ineffective. Are not all these proposals simply hollow words which have not changed anything for hundreds of years?

This objection has often been raised, and it deserves an answer. In the final analysis, the Church has only one instrument that is unique: the Gospel. Any other instrument would not only prove to be ineffective, but it would dilute the Church's faithfulness to her commission. Wherever the Church faithfully proclaims the Gospel and demonstrates the love it produces, great things will happen. The abolition of slavery in the last century is an excellent example of what dedicated Christians can accomplish in the world through the power of the Gospel.

If in fact it is true that not enough of the world's social ills have been changed through the efforts of the Church, the reason for it is not that the Church has depended too much on the power of the Gospel. It is rather that the Church has been one "of little faith" and has expected too little of the Gospel.

A renewal is needed. The power of the Holy Spirit working in the Church of Christ and her members needs to be unleashed. With repentance, faith and devotion, Christians can and will make their practical contribution in the solution of racism and to the other social evils of this sinful world.

Notes

CHAPTER 1. BIBLICAL HERMENEUTICS: THE STARTING POINT

1. *Drafts for Sections Prepared for the Fourth Assembly of the World Council of Churches,* Geneva, World Council of Churches, 1967, p. 10.
2. Gerhard Ebeling, "Die Bedeutung der historisch-kritische Methode für die protestantische Theologie und Kirche," *Zeitschrift für Theologie und Kirche,* Vol. 47, 1950, pp. 1-46.
3. Ernst Troeltsch, "Uber historische und dogmatische Methode in der Theologie," in *Gesammelte Schriften II,* Tübingen, J. D. B. Mohr (Paul Siebeck ,1913), pp. 729-753.

CHAPTER 2. THE STRUGGLE FOR SPIRITUAL IDENTITY

1. Bericht des Vorsitzenden des Rates der Evangelischen Kirche in Deutschland, Berlin-Spandau 1971, (mimeographed), p. 15. See also *Evangelische Kommentare* Vol. IV, No. 4, March 1971, pp. 121-123, S. Daecke, "Fehlalarm."
2. Rudolph Bultmann, ed., *Kerygma und Mythos,* Hamburg, Herbert Reich, 1960.
3. *Ibid.,* pp. 4-5.
4. Joachim Kahl, *The Misery of Christianity: A Plea for Humanism Without God,* Baltimore, Penguin Books, 1972, p. 104.
5. Mimeographed minutes of a working group, which formed part of a university seminar on Mission led by Prof. H. J. Margull in the summer term of 1970, p. 4. Cf. *International Review of Missions.* LX, 237, January, 1971, p. 18 and pp. 50ff.

CHAPTER 3. SHARPENING DEFINITIONS IN MISSION

1. *Drafts for Sections Prepared for the Fourth Assembly of the World Council of Churches,* Geneva, World Council of Churches, 1967.
2. Norman Goodall, ed., *Missions Under the Cross,* London, Edinburgh House Press, 1953, p. 188.
3. W. A. Visser 't Hooft, ed., *The Evanston Report,* London, SCM Press, 1955, p. 99.
4. John R. W. Stott, "Does Section Two Provide Sufficient Emphasis on World Evangelism?" *Eye of the Storm, The*

Great Debate in Mission, Donald McGavran, ed., Waco, Word Books, p. 268.

CHAPTER 4. THE CRUCIAL ISSUE OF MISSION AND HUMANIZATION

1. This concept has been clearly articulated by Prof. C. Peter Wagner of the Fuller Seminary faculty in a recent book, *Frontiers in Missionary Strategy,* (Chicago, Moody Press, 1971). See especially Chapter 2, "Biblical Principles for a Strategy of Missions."
2. Harold Lindsell, ed., *The Church's Worldwide Mission,* Waco, Word Books, 1966, pp. 228-229.
3. *Drafts for Sections Prepared for the Fourth Assembly of the World Council of Churches,* Geneva, World Council of Churches, 1967, p. 30.
4. McGavran's influential article bearing this title was first published in *Church Growth Bulletin,* Donald McGavran, ed., Vol. IV, No. 5, May, 1968, and later reprinted in the recent book, *Eye of the Storm, The Great Debate in Mission,* Donald McGavran, ed., Waco, Word Books, 1972, pp. 233-241.
5. John R. W. Stott, "Does Section Two Provide Sufficient Emphasis on World Evangelism?", *Church Growth Bulletin, Volumes I-V,* Donald McGavran, ed., South Pasadena, William Carey Library, 1969, p. 330.
6. N. Sithole, *African Nationalism,* Capetown, OUP, 1959.
7. Norman Goodall, ed., *The Uppsala Report 1968,* Geneva, World Council of Churches, 1968, p. 32.
8. Douglas Webster, *Bible and Mission,* London, British and Foreign Bible Society, 1970, p. 3.
9. This quotation is taken from the mimeographed minutes, p. 4, of a University Seminar on Mission led by Prof. Hans J. Margull in the summer of 1970.
10. *Ibid.,* pp. 3-4.
11. Cf. Ernst Bloch, *Atheismus im Christentum,* Suhrkamp Verlag, 1968.
12. Karl Marx, "Uber die Differenz der demokritischen und epikureischen Naturphilosophie," in *Frühe Schriften I,* H. J. Lieber and P. Furth, eds., Darmstadt, 1962, p. 3.
13. *Drafts for Sections . . . , op. cit.,* p. 34.

CHAPTER 5. THE STORY OF THE FRANKFURT DECLARATION

1. Peter Beyerhaus, *Missions: Which Way?,* Grand Rapids, Zondervan, 1971, p. 104.

CHAPTER 6. OPPORTUNITIES AND DANGERS IN ASIA

1. Peter Beyerhaus, "Unsere Mitverantwortung für die Kirchen Asiens in der ökumenischen Krise," in Evangelische Sammlung in Württemberg, Informationen, March, 1972, p. 3.
2. Harold Lindsell, ed., *The Church's Worldwide Mission,* Waco, Word Books, 1966, p. 231.
3. C. Peter Wagner, ed., *Church/Mission Tensions Today,* Chicago, Moody Press, 1972.

CHAPTER 7. MISSIONS AND RACISM

1. Tom Skinner, *Black and Free,* Grand Rapids, Zondervan Books, 1968, pp. 30-31.
2. *Ibid.,* p. 143.